THE GAP OF THE NORTH

ACKNOWLEDGEMENTS

This project has taken a long time to complete since its inception way back in the winter of 1999. While I have taken on the responsibility for the coordination and finishing of the publication, there have been many people in the background only too willing to lend a hand and help out. My sincere thanks go to these people, who have endured many deadlines, queries and instructions, including Pat McGinn and Noreen Cunningham who undertook the original research and writing of the book and Dr Ann Hamlin, who pulled the book together and was responsible for the initial edit. Also to the the staff of The O'Brien Press who have been patient and willing to take a risk with this book. Many of the photographs were taken by myself, but I would like to thank Sean Boylan, Tony Corey (EHS), Christopher Hill Photography and Dúchas who have provided additional images. My thanks also to John Marshall for the wonderful illustrations and to Victor Buckley, Dúchas who kindly allowed reproduction of the line drawings included in this book.

I would also like to thank our sponsors who have supported this publication and assisted in its quality production, including Dr Charles Mount, The Heritage Council; Dr Chris Lynn, The Environment and Heritage Service (NI); Miceal McCoy and Donna McSorley, LEADER II; Paula, Michelle and the Board of SATI, without whom none of this would have been possible. My final words of thanks go to Liam Hannaway without whom the project would not have started, and to Ross Millar (EHS) for his constant support and advice over the last few years.

Anthony Cranney

THE GAP OF THE NORTH

THE ARCHAEOLOGY & FOLKLORE OF ARMAGH, DOWN, LOUTH AND MONAGHAN

NOREEN CUNNINGHAM · PAT MCGINN

THE O'BRIEN PRESS
DUBLIN

This edition published 2001 by The O'Brien Press Ltd,
20 Victoria Road, Dublin 6, Ireland.
Tel: +353 1 4923333; Fax: +353 1 4922777
E-mail: books@obrien.ie
Website: www.obrien.ie

ISBN: 0-86278-707-6

British Library Cataloguing-in-Publication Data
A catalogue reference for this title is available from the British Library

1 2 3 4 5 6 7 8 9 10
01 02 03 04 05 06 07

The O'Brien Press receives
assistance from

the arts
council
an chomhairle
ealaíon
50

Editing, typesetting, layout and design: The O'Brien Press Ltd.
Maps: Design Image
Colour separations: C&A Print Services Ltd.
Printing: Leinster Leader

Picture Credits and Copyrights
Maps are reproduced courtesy of Ordnance Survey of Northern Ireland ©
Crown Copyright, Permit number 1605; photographs for site numbers
4, 6, 9, 10, 11, 13, 14, 15, 29 and illustration for site number 30 reproduced courtesy of
DOE(NI), the Environment and Heritage Service © Crown Copyright Reserved; for
site number 22 reproduced courtesy of Armagh City & District Council; photographs
for site numbers 5, 17, 19, 23 by Christopher Hill Photography
© South Armagh Tourism Initiative.
This publication received assistance from:

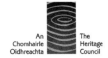

THE AUTHORS

NOREEN CUNNINGHAM is the curator of the Newry and
Mourne Museum. An Archaeology and Social Anthropology
graduate from Queen's University, Belfast (1984–1988),
Ms Cunningham also did a research fellowship on the
industrial heritage of Northern Ireland. Between 1989 and
1995 she worked with EHS (the Environment and Heritage
Service) as a consultant archaeologist and was involved in both
desk-based and field research for archaeological and industrial
sites. She has completed field studies of over 4,000 ancient
monuments. Subsequently she worked as a consultant
archaeologist on environmental impact studies and projects for
the Newry and Mourne District Council. She currently sits on
two committees for the Council and advises them on heritage
issues.

PAT McGINN is a local historian and folklore collector. A
graduate in Irish Studies from Queen's University, Belfast, he
also holds a Higher Diploma in Irish Folklore from University
College, Dublin. He has been involved in local history in the
area for many years, has written many newspaper articles about
the area and is currently facilitator and course tutor for an
NCVA (National Council of Vocational Awards) in local
folklore. The folklore project involves three centres from across
the province: Oideas Gael, Donegal; Ti Chulainn Cultural
Activity Centre, Mullaghbane; and the YMCA in Newcastle,
Co Down. Mr McGinn is a recognised WEA (Workers
Education Awards) tutor and a member of the Ti Chulainn
Committee as well as the Camlough Historical Society. He
previously worked as education assistant at the Slieve Gullion
Courtyard Centre and as a journalist with various local
newspapers.

Contents

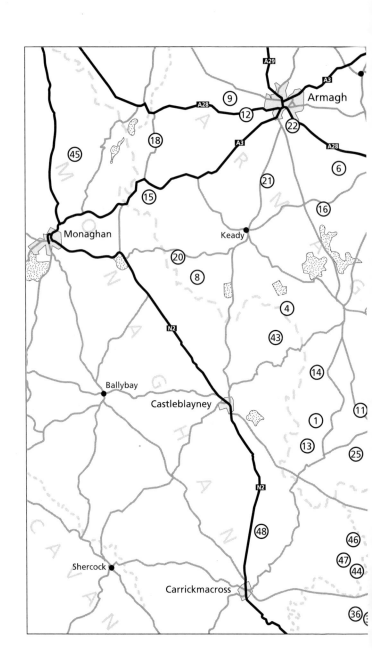

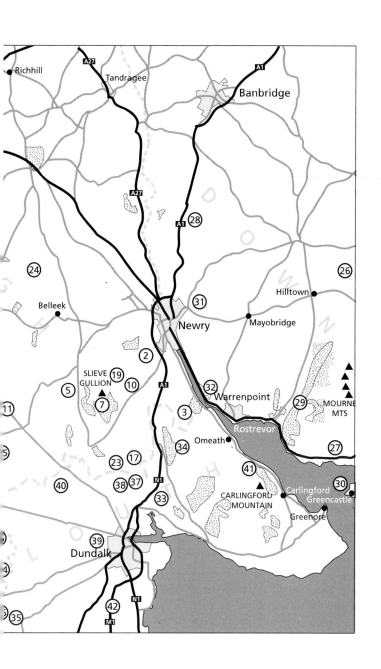

INTRODUCTION

Man has lived in Ireland for over 9,000 years. In the study area — The Gap of the North — we have ample evidence in the form of stone and earthwork monuments for occupation since the Neolithic period (New Stone Age 5,000BC–2,000BC). There is, however, other archaeological evidence not easily visible on the surface which indicates that man has been here for much longer.

While there is no real evidence of the Palaeolithic period (Old Stone Age) in Ireland, a single Palaeolithic flint flake was recovered from a quarry near Drogheda, Co Louth. Despite this unusual discovery it is generally accepted that the earliest human activity in Ireland began during the Mesolithic (Middle Stone Age).

Man could not easily have lived in Ireland before the Mesolithic period because the country was largely covered by deep ice sheets known as glaciers. Climactic change made settlement possible only around 12,000 years ago, when the glaciers retreated and a lush meadowland replaced the once frozen tundra landscape. Early in this new post-glacial period, Ireland remained joined to Britain and it is possible that some of the first settlers used this landbridge to cross to Ireland. As the climate warmed, sea levels rose, and Ireland became a true island.

These first people arrived in Ireland over 9,000 years ago and settled around the north and east coast. It is here that shell middens, hearths and flint tools have been found. These early communities are thought to have lived a hunter-gatherer lifestyle and moved around in family groups, utilising the available seasonal resources. Settlement appears to have been concentrated around the coast and along riverbanks and lakeshores. One of the best-known Mesolithic sites in Ireland is Mount Sandel, Co Derry, situated at the mouth of the River Bann, upstream from Coleraine. Mesolithic material has also been found inland, along the shores of Lough Neagh. However, we have as yet no evidence for Mesolithic settlement in our study area.

The Neolithic (New Stone Age)

About 6,000 years ago a new wave of settlers arrived in Ireland, journeying across the sea in boats from Britain and the continent. These Neolithic farmers brought with them new tools, pottery and a settled way of life which was made possible by agriculture. They also brought new seed, corn and domestic breeds of cattle, pig, sheep and goat. They appear to have settled in upland areas where the woodland was less dense and soon set about clearing woodlands and laying out fields. Remnants of these ancient field walls are found at the Ceide Fields complex in Co Mayo where they were discovered during peat cutting.

The first farmers forged extensive trade networks. Stone axes from rock outcrops at Tievebulliagh near Cushendall in Co Antrim and Brockley on Rathlin Island were sent out along trade routes as far afield as southern England. While habitation sites are rare, the enduring legacy of the Neolithic farmers is their burial monuments, the megalithic tombs. As they were constructed of stone, they have a naturally greater survival rate than settlement sites and it is in these stone monuments that we find pottery, flint tools and items of personal adornment. Through much of Ireland four classes of tomb are found: Court Tombs, Passage Tombs, Portal Tombs and Wedge Tombs. Broadly chronological in sequence, this is not a hard and fast rule and there is some overlap in time between tomb types.

Court Tombs are the earliest tomb type and many are found around the Gap of the North. They are usually covered by the remains of a stone cairn which normally tapers from front to back, giving them a 'trapezoidal' or wedge-shaped appearance. To the front of the tomb is an unroofed court area

A reconstruction drawing of a court tomb covered with a cairn

defined by large upright stones, known as orthostats. Inside the tombs there are stone-lined chambers where the burials were deposited. Most tombs had one or two chambers in linear arrangement, while others had up to four.

Finds from the tombs have yielded leaf- and lozenge-shaped flint arrowheads, hollow scrapers and undecorated round-bottomed bowls. Sometimes ornaments and food offerings are also found, but the scarcity of these items contrasts with the large numbers of beads and pendants found in Passage graves or tombs.

Passage Tombs appear to date from around 2,500BC, when a new wave of tomb builders crossed the channel from Brittany. Passage tombs are found not only in Ireland but also on the Menai Straits between Anglesey and the mainland of Wales and in the north of France. The best-known Irish example of a passage tomb is at Newgrange, Co Meath. In form these tombs have burial chambers of cruciform shape, generally found deep inside a mound or stone cairn, approached by a passageway. They are frequently located on hilltops, and while the examples in our region are single examples, they also appear in groups.

There are several passage tombs in the study area, the best preserved is located on the summit of Slieve Gullion (7), and at 574m is the highest surviving megalith of its type in the British Isles. These tombs usually contain stones which are elaborately decorated with spirals, zigzags, triangles, circles, stylized faces and other abstract designs. Early archaeological reports of Carnavanaghan Passage Tomb, known as The Vicar's Cairn (6) record inscribed or carved stones, suggesting passage tomb art. None are found at the site today which means that they have either been removed by antiquarians or destroyed for local building purposes. Cremated remains of the dead were deposited in shallow stone basins – usually accompanied by decorated pottery called Carrowkeel ware – personal ornaments and curious stone and chalk objects.

Portal Tombs became more common in the late Neolithic era.

Characterised by an impressive entrance, portal tombs have a single chamber, roofed with a large capstone. They are usually set into the end of an earthen long barrow, though in many instances this feature has been eroded. There is a close similarity between finds in court and portal tombs and it is possible that portal tombs have structural links with the earlier court tombs, illustrated by the portal tomb at Goward Dolmen (26). The massive capstone resting on two portals and backstone has caused speculation about tomb construction techniques. It is thought that ramps of earth were constructed and the capstone was dragged into position using a pulley system.

Unburned human bones recovered from these tombs indicate that inhumation was practised, as it was in the court tombs, though cremations were common. Finds from the tombs include hollow flint scrapers, arrowheads and decorated pots. There are a number of impressive portal tombs in our area; they include Ballykeel Dolmen (5) in South Armagh, which retains remains of a long cairn, Kilfeaghan Dolmen (27) in Co Down, where a glacial erratic seems to have been reused as a capstone, and Goward Dolmen (26).

Wedge Tombs are of a late Neolithic – early Bronze Age date. It has been argued that they may have been introduced from western France. Fine Beaker ware has been found in wedge tombs, but mainly in the north of the country. In general, wedge tombs occur singly, and although the siting of the tomb varies, the main distribution is on high pastureland where the underlying rock is limestone or sandstone.

Wedge tombs, as their name implies, are easily recognised by their distinctive shape, sloping downward from front to rear and narrowing towards the back. A small heel-shaped cairn often surrounds the tomb. Inside, communal burials are frequently found, and both inhumation and cremation rites were practised. Pottery and flints were the main grave goods, with wrist guards also found in some tombs. There are no known examples of this tomb type in counties Armagh or Down, but a wedge tomb is found beside Proleek Dolmen (33) in Co Louth.

THE BRONZE AGE (2,000BC–500BC)

The Bronze Age is a period in prehistory when people first began to identify and locate metal ores to make weapons, tools and ornaments. The ability to work copper seems to have spread from southern Turkey west into Europe. Knowledge of metalworking reached Britain and Ireland around 2,000BC, heralding the end of the Neolithic Age. These early metallurgists are associated with a distinctive type of domestic pottery known as Beaker Ware. The earliest metal objects were made from copper, which contained traces of arsenic. It is believed that this gave copper strength. Soon true bronze – an alloy of copper and tin – was being produced.

The tiny daggers, bronze bracelets and javelin heads found in graves were not of much functional use and were more likely items of prestige, owned by a wealthy few. It was not long before practical objects such as flat axes were being produced in considerable numbers. These metal tools were superior to their polished stone predecessors and soon took over as the weapon of choice. Later in the Bronze Age weapons such as swords, rapiers and spearheads were cast in moulds of fired clay, which were broken open to extract the item. Such moulds have been unearthed at The King's Stables (9), near Navan Fort.

Bronze Age copper mines and evidence of copper smelting have been found at Mount Gabriel in Co Cork and at Ross Island near Killarney, Co Kerry. Copper deposits are also found at Tullyvallen, near Silverbridge. However, no evidence has been unearthed to prove that these were being used at this time. These early metalworkers also made objects from gold panned from the streambeds in areas such as Co Wicklow and Co Tyrone. Round gold discs, earrings, torcs, dress fasteners and crescentic collars or lunalae were made by craftsmen and worn by a wealthy section of the populace. Many of these items have been found in bogs, rivers and lakes, and were probably ritually deposited.

Field monuments of this period are less obvious to the untrained eye than the massive megaliths of the Neolithic, and include rock art (petroglyphs), standing stones, ceremonial stone circles and alignments, earthworks such as Haughey's Fort and ritual pools like The King's Stables (9), both located near Navan Fort (12). The prevalent burial mode was interment in a cist, a small rectangular pit lined and roofed with stone slabs. Inside the cist a crouched inhumation burial or cremated remains are usually discovered, accompanied by a food vessel or cinerary urn. Sometimes a mound or cairn was heaped over the cist, such as found on the northern summit of Slieve Gullion (7).

Rock art of this period is usually found on earthfast boulders and rock outcrops and consists of circular depressions carved into the rock surface. Sometimes they are enclosed by concentric circles and are termed 'cup and ring' marks. Rock art may have had a religious or ritual significance to Bronze Age society but it has been speculated that it may also have had an educational purpose; perhaps for studying the stars or mapping. In Ireland the greatest concentration of rock art is in counties Cork and Kerry. In the north of the country, however, distribution is sparse, with examples found in northwest Louth, extending southwest into Co Monaghan, at Drumirill (44). There are no examples in Co Armagh and only a few in Co Down. A stone with a cup and ring mark was found in the bank of a rath outside Hilltown and is now in the Ulster Museum.

Standing stones are another somewhat enigmatic monument. Excavations have sometimes uncovered burials, while others may have simply functioned as route markers. Other examples may be the remnants of a megalith, while the situation is further confused by the erection of stone scratching posts in the eighteenth and nineteenth centuries. There are many fine examples of standing stones in Co Down around Burren and Mayobridge. Other good examples are the Long Stone at Ballard, Co Armagh and the 'Cú Chulainn Stone' at Knockbridge, Co Louth.

Habitation sites from this period are very rare and one of the best-known in the study area is a lakeside settlement excavated at Cullyhanna Lough. Consisting of an enclosure defined by a timber palisade and containing a circular house, it was dated by dendrochronolgy (tree rings study) to 1526BC.

Other sites of a broadly Bronze Age date are burnt mounds or 'Fulacht Fiadh'. They are usually found near a water source and were cooking places. A wooden trough was filled with water and heated stones thrown in. When the water was hot the stones were raked out and wrapped bundles of meat were placed in the trough to cook. The stones formed kidney-shaped mounds which characterise these sites. There are a number of these sites in Co Louth.

THE IRON AGE (500BC–AD500)

The next progression in metalworking was the utilisation of iron; this is commonly identified with a movement of Celtic peoples from Central Europe into Ireland. The Iron Age is sometimes referred to as the 'dawn of history' and is often associated with the heroic figures of Finn McCool and *Cú Chulainn*. People of the Iron Age used iron mainly for their weapons, and bronze objects — especially prestige items — were still being produced during this period. Iron, unlike bronze, is more prone to destruction, especially from rust, so what does survive in the archaeological record is only a small fraction of what once existed.

Sites most readily identified with the Iron Age include hillforts, which are more commonly found in the southern part of the country. One of the most famous is the massive hillfort at Mooghaun in Co Clare, which covers 12.5 hectares. There are a few similar sites in the area but on a much smaller scale; these include the hilltop enclosure at Faughart Upper, Co Louth, or Haughey's Fort, near Navan Fort.

Some of the chief sites associated with the Iron Age in our area are Navan Fort (12) and the linear earthworks which travel across the northern part of the country. Known as The Dane's Cast (10) in

Co Armagh and Co Down and The Black Pig's Dyke in Co Monaghan, these monuments are discontinuous lines of bank and ditch. The Dorsey (11) in South Armagh is a massive linear earthwork that controlled a major route into Ulster.

A number of artefacts of Iron Age date have been found in the study area; they include a massive bronze armlet of Scottish design found in Newry, now in the National Museum in Dublin, and the Tandragee Idol — a horned or helmeted enigmatic figure clutching his shoulder — found outside Newry, now held in St Patrick's Church of Ireland Cathedral, Armagh.

The Early Christian Period (AD500–AD1200)

Following on from the Iron Age, with little cultural interruption, is the Early Christian Period. It was a time of great artistic achievement, with metalwork, manuscript painting and sculpture attaining great heights of excellence. There is a wealth of monuments dating from this era, including raths, cashels, souterrains, crannogs and ecclesiastical sites.

Raths (also called ringforts, lios, forts, dun and cathairs), are the most commonly found field monuments in Ireland. Some 30–40,000 raths are known, and every townland may have had one. It is possible that the origins of many of our townlands date from this time. Raths are often referred to in the Irish Sagas and other writings and it is clear that they were dwelling places, at least of the better-off strata of society. It is impossible to relate the findings of excavation at these sites directly to literary accounts, even when an individual rath can be reliably identified.

Raths were built primarily to house a farming family and some livestock. They are usually oval in plan with an earth bank and outer ditch. The interior or habitation area usually measures about 30m in diameter. Larger sites with two or more sets of banks and ditches may indicate a higher status inhabitant, these are known as multivallate raths. In South Armagh there are several good examples of multivallate raths, they include the trivallate raths at Lisleitrim Fort (14) and Rathtrillick (15) and the exceptionally well-preserved bivallate rath at Corliss Fort (13).

Cashels are similar in age and function to raths, but have an enclosing wall built of stone. They are usually found in areas where soil is thin and bedrock is easily accessible. There is a marked concentration of cashels outside Newry, in the Fathom and Flagstaff area and around Mayobridge, Co Down. The walls are usually several metres thick and they have a clearly defined entrance.

Souterrains (also known as caves) are underground tunnels that are often associated with raths, cashels and ecclesiastical sites. Co Louth has one of the highest concentrations of souterrains in Ireland, in the area between the Castletown and Fane Rivers. Many of those in Louth have no accompanying rath or cashel and this has led some archaeologists to suggest that there may also have been another type of habitation site in this area, perhaps unenclosed house sites. In our area the ecclesiastical sites of Killevy and Donaghmore both have recorded souterrains. It is thought that souterrains were used as refuges in times of unrest, such as cattle- or slave-raiding and later to hide from Vikings, but it is also possible that they were used to store farm produce like milk or grain.

Crannogs are artificial islands built as defended settlements. They are sometimes found in close proximity to large raths such as at Lisleitrim (14) and at Corliss (13). Deposits of stone and wood were dumped in a shallow place in a lake, creating a level platform on

A reconstruction drawing of a crannog

which houses were built. The material was usually surrounded by a palisade of timber stakes which served as a restraint to hold the island together. Access to crannogs was by boat or canoe, and in some instances submerged causeways of stone were also used.

Churches Lastly, but perhaps most importantly, mention should be made of an integral part of Early Christian society – the church. We know from writings that there were Christians in Ireland before the arrival of St Patrick in AD460, but it was Patrick who laid the foundations for Christianity in Ireland. The first churches were probably small timber structures with a high pitched roof and later they were rebuilt using stone. Many of the monasteries and convents at this time were self-sufficient units. They were large enclosures, with the church and the living quarters in the centre, and vegetable and herb gardens, an area for crafts and accommodation for travellers situated near the entrance gate. Important religious centres include Armagh (22), which was plundered on several occasions by the Vikings; Killevy (19), Inishkeen (46) and Louth (36).

Monuments from this period include cross-carved pillar stones such as Kilnasaggart (17), and stone crosses, which start to appear from the seventh or eight century onwards; examples of these can be found at Kilbroney (29), and Donaghmore (28). These freestanding crosses served many purposes; they often marked the entrance to monasteries, or burial places of important clerics. From the tenth century onwards the 'scripture crosses' became common; good examples are the crosses at Donaghmore (28) and Tynan (18) and there are also cross fragments in St Patrick's Cathedral, Armagh, and at Faughart (37). Scripture crosses have carved images reflecting passages from both the old and the new testaments and it is thought that they were used as a pictorial means of transmitting the bible. Later crosses found in the area include the medieval high cross at Donagh in Co Monaghan (45), which features a carved crucified figure.

Round Towers are also a common symbol of the early Irish church. The earliest of these are thought to date from the latter part of the ninth century and continued to be built up until the twelfth century. It is thought that they were built by the monasteries to protect their clerics and their wealth, in response to Viking raids. As the door of the tower was located well above the ground surface, access to the tower was via a ladder. The best-preserved tower in our area is the picturesquely sited Inishkeen Round Tower (46) although others are thought to have stood at Killevy (19) and Faughart (37).

THE MIDDLE AGES

The coming of the Anglo-Normans in the twelfth century heralded major upheavals and changes in Ireland, particularly in political and ecclesiastical matters. A new monument type – the motte and bailey – starts to appear with the initial conquests. In south Down and Louth mottes were built in strategic locations. One of the best-preserved is the somewhat overgrown Crown Mound (31) on the outskirts of Newry, while other examples are found at Hilltown, Dún Dealgan (39) and Candlefort; Inishkeen (47). Mottes functioned as sites of control and defence, and were flat-topped mounds, usually with an accompanying lower mound – the bailey. The first castles built on the mottes were of wood, but stronger castles of stone, such as Mannan Castle (48) near Donaghmoyne, were erected later. The bailey, also surrounded by a ditch, was usually rectangular in shape and functioned as a base for troops and retainers.

Soon after the initial invasion, prominent Norman lords built impressive stone castles requiring much in terms of resources. They served as strong-points of control and power. In our area we have the particularly fine examples of King John's Castle at Carlingford (41), Greencastle (30) and Castle Roche (40).

Changes in the church were beginning to appear even before the Norman Conquest. It has been said that the twelfth century was the period of greatest change since the advent of Christianity. On the continent new religious orders such as the Cistercians, Augustinians, Dominicans and Franciscans were formed. Contact between clergy in Ireland, Britain and the continent meant that change was inevitable. In 1142 one of the leading clerics of the day, St Malachy of Armagh (22), visited St Bernard of Clairvaux and asked him to send some of his monks to Ireland. The Cistercians settled at Mellifont in 1142 and from there sent out monks to other sites, most notably to Newry, where they arrived in 1153. These new orders reformed the older established Irish religious communities, and replaced the unplanned layouts with regimented precision. All buildings now radiated out from a central courtyard area, with the church on the north side, kitchen and refectory on the south and the monks' accommodation on the upper floors.

In the late medieval period a type of castle called a 'tower house' appears. Smaller and less imposing than the earlier Norman castles, these were initially built to protect the Pale, but were soon erected throughout the country. They were initiated by a subsidy of £10 offered by King Henry VI in 1429. Tower houses were usually rectangular in shape, with three to five storeys, a thatched roof, machiolation over the doorway, wall-walk at roof level, murder holes, and loops for arrows and guns. Some had external towers for the stairs and latrines and enclosing bawn. In our area there are few tower houses, with probably the best example at Dunmahon (42) and the recently rediscovered Bagenal's Castle in Newry. In Armagh there are few surviving remains, with fragmentary remains of an O'Neill tower house at Middletown and only documentary references to the tower house that once stood at Glassdrumman.

THE PLANTATION 1600

During the early Plantation period, as the English tried to assert power and control over the northern counties of Ireland, they built highly defensive castles such as Moyry Castle (23) and modified existing earthworks such as Faughart Motte (38) as they moved north through south Armagh. Just north of the study area, Charles Blount, Lord Deputy Mountjoy, who erected Moyry Castle, built a massive star-shaped fort at Charlemont on the banks of the River Blackwater in 1602. It stationed 150 men and was the most significant piece of military architecture built in the area during the Plantation period. These rare examples of military architecture are the final part of our look at The Gap of the North region. The built heritage of the region does not stop in the early seventeenth century, but archaeology was superceded by architecture and new styles of building as new urban towns and villages developed under the watchful eye of landlords and planters.

Enjoy this glimpse into the wondrous and eventful past which has endowed our landscape with such a rich array of archaeological monuments. As you explore this region remember that what we see now in the archaeological record is just a fraction of what was once there.

HOW TO USE THIS GUIDE

The Gap of the North is a field guide which will help you to understand some of the region's best known archaeological monuments and a few lesser known gems. The book is broken into four different sections, each dealing with a different county: Armagh, Down, Louth and Monaghan. The monuments in each of these sections are then looked at chronologically, starting with the earliest monument types and ending with the more recent additions to our monument record.

Each entry is clearly numbered (1–48) which, for the purposes of this book, refer to the monument reference number. These numbers are consistent with each entry and can be referred to on the enclosed map or in any relevant photographic references. Each entry includes a main body of text which describes the archaeological features and any history or folklore relating to the site, and gives source material references, which are fully detailed in the Bibliography. It also includes the following information: Monument Type; Location; Grid Reference; Monument Number and Status.

MONUMENT TYPE

This heading classifies the monument into a monument type recognised by the major archaeological institutes. In general they classify the monument as a simple type, e.g. castle or cairn. A more detailed description of the monument and any associated history, folklore or mythology is included in the main text.

LOCATION

The location of each monument is given in relation to the nearest town, village or significant landmark. The monuments are clearly numbered on the map on page 8 which shows the counties, main roads and nearest major town. The map is not designed for the purposes of navigation and it is recommended that you use the 1:50,000 scale

Ordnance Survey Discovery Series Maps: Sheet 19 (Armagh), Sheet 28 (Monaghan), Sheet 29 (Mourne), Sheet 36A (Carlingford Lough), or, alternatively, you could use the 1:70,000 scale map entitled 'The Gateway to Ulster' which covers the entire area.

GRID REFERENCE

The grid references given are standard with normal grid reference guidelines and can be used on the above-mentioned Ordnance Survey Discovery Series Maps to help with navigation and location of monuments.

MONUMENT NUMBER

Each monument in both Northern Ireland and The Republic of Ireland is protected. Each of these monuments has its own unique reference number, which is included in this guide. The reference number is particularly useful if you wish to research any of the monuments in this book or if you simply want more information. In Northern Ireland this reference number has been allocated by the Environment & Heritage Service (Department of the Environment for Northern Ireland). More information on monuments in Northern Ireland can be found in the Monuments and Buildings Record (MBR), 5-33 Hill Street, Belfast. The MBR has data on over 14,500 archaeological sites and holds over 50,000 publicly accessible black and white photographs. Access is free, but visitors should consult with MBR staff before any visit to arrange their requirements. In the Republic of Ireland all monuments have been recorded in the Record of Monuments and Places (RMP). The RMP was established under a section of the National Monuments (Amendment) Act, 1994. A record has been drawn up for each county and gives each monument listed a measure of protection. The RMP number is preceded by the standard county abbreviation; LH(Louth), MN (Monaghan).

STATUS

The heritage of Ireland is very special and both the Environment & Heritage Service in Northern Ireland and Dúchas, The Heritage Service in the Republic of Ireland, have put in place measures to ensure the preservation and protection of the country's archaeological record.

In Northern Ireland there are three categories of protection:

1. State Care Monuments: which accounts for 181 monuments in Northern Ireland. These are usually owned and maintained by the state and most are accessible to the public.

2. Scheduled Historic Monuments: which are normally in private ownership and have no formal access arrangements. Some graveyards fall into this category and are easily accessible, but other monuments in the countryside are not. It is important to ensure that you agree access to these sites with the landowner.

3. Recorded Historic Monuments: by law it is an offence to damage or interfere with any monument in Northern Ireland.

In the Republic Of Ireland protection of archaeology is facilitated under the revised European Union Convention on the Protection of Archaeological Heritage (1992). Historic monuments are legally protected by inclusion in the Register of Historic Monuments, which includes all monuments in existence before AD1700 or such later date as the Minister may appoint by regulations.

The Register of Historic Monuments lists known sites and areas which are considered to be of archaeological importance and it is an offence to 'demolish or remove wholly or in part or disfigure, deface, alter or in any manner interfere with a historic monument that is entered in the Register'. For more details on the Register of Historic Monuments contact Dúchas, The Heritage Service at 6 Ely Place Upper, Dublin 2; Tel: +01 6473000; e-mail duchas@ealga.ie

GLOSSARY

Archaeology The scientific study of the material remains of past human life and activities. These include human artefacts and structures, from the very earliest bones and stone tools to the present day. Archaeological investigations are the principal source of knowledge of prehistoric, ancient, and extinct cultures.

Bailey The outer courtyard of a castle, enclosed by earthwork banks or stone walls.

Barrel Vault A continuous vault, or stone roof, which is either semicircular or pointed in profile.

Bawn A walled enclosure, usually around or attached to a house or castle.

Bivallate A term often applied to raths which have two surrounding earthen banks or ramparts and ditches.

Buttress A masonry structure to give extra support to a wall.

Cairn A pile of stones used as a boundary marker, a memorial, or a burial site, often erected on high ground. Burial cairns date primarily from the Neolithic and the Early Bronze Ages, and often covered Neolithic tombs.

Capstone A large, usually flat, stone used to cover a chamber, of, for example, a Neolithic portal tomb or a souterrain.

Cashel Similar to raths, cashels are early circular farmsteads which used available stones instead of earthen banks for the circular defensive drystone walls. Cashels are usually found in rocky areas where the soils are thin.

Causeway A raised walkway or road.

Chancel The eastern part of a church where the main altar is found, usually reserved for the clergy and the choir.

Cist A stone coffin which contains bones or ashes, also applied to an underground, slab-built burial chamber covered with a flat slab.

Court Tomb The earliest type of megalithic tomb in Ireland, so called because of the semicircular open space, or court, in front of the burial gallery.

Crannog Found mainly in Scotland and Ireland, these are artificially constructed settlement sites in lakes, made of timber and stone.

Curtain Wall A defensive wall surrounding a castle.

Dendrochronology Tree-ring dating is the scientific discipline concerned with dating and interpreting past events, particularly paleoclimates and climatic trends, based on the analysis of the growth rings of trees.

Dolmen A megalithic monument formed by a large capstone supported by upright stones, known as a portal tomb.

Earthwork A monument made of

earth, usually for defensive mounds, banks and ramparts.

Excavation The scientific uncovering and recording of monuments, carried out in the contexts of research and rescue.

Façade Outward visible surface, of a building or monument, often applied to the front.

Gallery In archaeology, this is an elongated stone-covered passage entered at one end, often associated with court tombs.

Gatehouse A defensive building, which protects the gateway, usually associated with castles.

Hall The main room in a castle or great house, where public events were held.

Keep A tower which serves as the central stronghold of a castle.

Latrine In military speak, a lavatory.

Machicolation A projecting gallery, usually made of stone, through which missiles and objects could be dropped on enemies. Associated with castles and tower-houses, they usually protected an entrance.

Megalith A prehistoric tomb or other structure made of large stones, from the Greek, *mega* (big) and *lithos* (stone).

Mesolithic Also called the Middle Stone Age, the cultural stage between the Palaeolithic, with its chipped stone tools, and the Neolithic, with its polished stone tools.

Motte A circular, high, steep-sided,

flat-topped, earthen mound on which a wooden tower was erected, associated with the advance of the Anglo-Normans in the late twelfth and thirteenth centuries (see also Bailey).

Multivallate Applied to a site, like a rath, with several banks and ditches.

Nave The western part of a church, where the lay people worshipped.

Neolithic Also called the New Stone Age, following the Mesolithic (qv), characterised by settled farming and the building of megalithic tombs.

Orthostats Large upright stones, for example those demarcating the court of a Neolithic court tomb (qv).

Palaeolithic Also called the Old Stone Age, the earliest stage of human development, characterised by the use of rudimentary chipped stone tools, followed by the Mesolithic (qv) in about 8,000BC.

Palisade A defensive wall of timber posts.

Passage Tomb A megalithic tomb type in which the burial chamber is approached by a passage, under a covering mound or cairn.

Portal Stones A pair of upright stones, supporting a capstone, forming the entrance to the burial chamber of a dolmen (qv).

Portal Ton

Rampart A stone wall, s by a palisade

Rath Circulai

an earthen bank, an enclosed homestead of the Early Christian period.

Ring barrow A burial surrounded by a circular bank of earth or stone dated to the Bronze or Iron Age.

Ringfort – See Rath.

Souterrain An underground chamber or passage used as a refuge and for storage in the Early Christian period.

Tracery The ornamental stonework in the head of a window, made up of curved and intersecting bars of stone.

Urn Vase-like pottery vessel often associated with Bronze Age burials.

Vault An arched roof, for example over a cellar or burial chamber or a tower-house (see also Barrel Vault).

① ANNAGHMARE COURT TOMB

MONUMENT TYPE	Court Tomb
LOCATION	Near Cullyhanna
GRID REFERENCE	H9049 1782
MONUMENT NUMBER	27:07
STATUS	State Care DOENI (EHS)

The megalithic tomb at Annaghmare – *Eanach Már,* the big marsh – has been described as one of the finest surviving court tombs in Northern Ireland. This tomb, which was built by early farming communities over 6,000 years ago, is a testament to their skills as monument builders. Located on a rocky knoll in a modern forestry plantation, and surrounded by low boggy ground, it is best approached along a path through the trees. The tomb, which is

Three stone-lined burial galleries at Annaghmare Court Tomb

known locally as 'The Black Castle', has been used for burials at various times in the Neolithic (New Stone) Age and is thought to have been used for unconsecrated burials in the more recent past.

The cairn, roughly rectangular in shape, is 20m long and encloses a three-chambered burial gallery. The tomb is entered from the south through a very fine forecourt, which is horseshoe-shaped, and exhibits finely executed post-and-panel drystone walling between the large upright stones known as orthostats. The enclosing cairn is exceptionally well preserved and excavations in 1962–3 revealed that it had also been extended to cover two lateral chambers to the north.

These two chambers are entered from the sides of the cairn. Because there was no retaining kerb at this end of the cairn the excavator concluded that further lengthening may have been planned, but was never carried out.

During excavation of the burial gallery chambers, Neolithic pottery, flint scrapers and a very fine javelin head were unearthed. The tomb also contained the unburnt skeletal remains of an adult female and a child, and a great deal of cremated bone. 'The Black Castle' has been the site of many local ghost sightings, perhaps a reminder of its eventful and ceremonial past.

Sources: Waterman D.M., *UJA* 28, 1965, 3-46.

② BALLYMACDERMOT CAIRN

MONUMENT TYPE	Court Tomb
LOCATION	Near the Bernish View Point, near Newry
GRID REFERENCE	J0656 2402
MONUMENT NUMBER	26:15
STATUS	State Care DOENI (EHS)

Ballymacdermot – *Bhaile Mhic Dhiarmada*, McDermot's townland – is a low mountain to the east of Slieve Gullion. Located on a level terrace on the southeastern slopes of the mountain is a well-preserved court tomb known as Ballymacdermot Cairn. From this site panoramic views over the plain of Meigh, Slieve Gullion and the ring dyke hills to the south can be enjoyed, a phenomenon that surely did not escape the early farming communities who built it over 6,000 years ago. Locally known as 'The Cashla', it is also spoken of as 'The Graves', and 'The Fairy Ring', and is reputed to be haunted.

A wedge-shaped cairn encloses the tomb, which is entered through a semicircular forecourt and a small antechamber. The tomb contains two stone-lined burial chambers which were once covered by 'large roofing stones', some of which still survive. Traces of the perimeter

Forecourt of Ballymacdermot Cairn

kerb are visible at the back and sides of the monument, but only rock outcrops to the front. Ballymacdermot Cairn has been investigated at various times in its history. In the nineteenth century it was opened by treasure-seekers, including John Bell of Killevy Castle, who unearthed an urn containing pulverised bone in one of the chambers. Mr Bell, writing in *The Newry Magazine* in 1816, described the chambered cairn of Ballymacdermot as a *tamlachta* or cairn.

More recently, during the Second World War, some of the façade stones were thrown down and broken by the American Army on tank manoeuvres. In 1962 the cairn was excavated and sherds of pottery and worked flints were recovered, but owing to the acidic nature of the soil, only a few fragments of cremated bone were found. After excavation the site was conserved, with fallen stones re-erected and broken ones repaired.

Folklorist George Paterson recorded the following story about a man who tried to destroy the tomb:

> Sur' he saw no hurt in the breakin' of it. But he never lived till finish it. For hundreds of years it has been there – maybe indeed since the beginning of time. I always remember it. Sure, it was there that I saw the first wee people.

Ancient Ballymacdermot was the property of the O'Hanlon

family, but during the Plantation of Ulster (1593–1603) it was granted by Queen Elizabeth I to Sir Marmaduke Whitechurch, who died in May 1635. His granddaughter, Eleanor Symonds, carried this townland into the Seaver family through her marriage to Nicholas Seaver of Ballyaghy, Co Armagh. Nicholas was the great-grandfather of Jonathan Seaver, one of the larger landlords in the area – known locally as 'Seaver of the Bog'. Ballymacdermot Cairn has seen many changes of land ownership and survived frequent attacks from greedy treasure-seekers. Against all the odds, it still stands today, watching over this unique landscape, protected surely by the 'little people'.

Sources: Collins A.E.P. & Wilson B.C.S., *UJA* 27, 1964, 3-22.

❸ CLONTYGORA COURT TOMB

MONUMENT TYPE	Court Tomb
LOCATION	Near the Flagstaff View Point, south of Newry
GRID REFERENCE	J0987 1945
MONUMENT NUMBER	29:11
STATUS	State Care DOENI (EHS)

Clontygora – *Chluainte Gabhra,* the meadow of the goats – is located at the foot of Anglesey Mountain overlooking the flat plains of Meigh towards Slieve Gullion. The court tomb, which is over 6,000 years old, is known locally as 'The King's Ring', and is an impressive monument despite damage in the past. In the eighteenth century stones were removed from the tomb to build the first lock on the Newry Canal, in the nineteenth century to construct the quay at Narrow Water, and in more recent years to build field boundary walls.

The forecourt is the most impressive feature of the tomb and is defined by very large upright stones known as orthostats. The tallest of these are near the centre of the forecourt and stand over 2.75m high. The ruined burial gallery consists of at least two, probably three, chambers and, as in Ballymacdermot Cairn (2), some roofing slabs still survive. Very little remains of the stone cairn which once would have covered the tomb, but the first burial chamber is quite well preserved and is almost 3m wide. Stone has been robbed from the second chamber, and also from a third chamber, leaving it with no existing surface remains at all; evidence of this third chamber was revealed only by excavation, the below-ground archaeological record showing evidence of burials and earlier stone structures. During excavation of the tomb in 1937 small fragments of human bone were recovered from the burial chambers, with Neolithic pottery and flint, including three fine leaf-shaped arrowheads.

'The King's Ring'

Folklorist George Paterson collected a story which recalls the once majestic tomb:

> The King's Ring was a grand place once, but they took stones to build the lock on Newry Canal. There was a time when there was music in the ring. It was quare music, one minute it would coax the heart out of you, and the next it would scare the living daylights out of you. Maybe it is laments for the oul' kings that are played.

Unlike many other ancient monuments, Clontygora Court Tomb

has not been completely destroyed by stone robbers and builders, and it stands as a reminder of our distant ancestors who first created and farmed the fields of south Armagh.

Sources: Davies O. and Paterson T.G.F. in *PBNHPS* I part 2, 1938, 20-42; Paterson T.G.F., 1945, 32.

❹ AUGHNAGURGAN DOLMEN

MONUMENT TYPE	Portal Tomb
LOCATION	Near Tullynawood Lake, Darkley
GRID REFERENCE	H8704 2859
MONUMENT NUMBER	24:02
STATUS	Scheduled Historic Monument

In a field high up in the Fews Mountains of south Armagh, one mile south of the tiny linen milling village of Darkley, is Aughnagurgan Dolmen. The now partly collapsed dolmen stands on a southwest-facing slope overlooking Tullynawood Lake and is commonly known as 'The Giant's Grave'.

The once table-like dolmen has, unfortunately, collapsed. It

The Children of Lir rest 'on the waters of fair Tullinawood'

The collapsed capstone has forced two of the upright stones to lean inwards

consists of four stones which once supported the large capstone, now slipped down from its original position. The fallen capstone has forced two of the upright stones to lean markedly inwards and is now broken. This may be the site referred to by John Bell, an antiquarian and treasure-seeker, in *The Newry Magazine* of 1816, when he described a 'very fine cairne or taimhleacht' in the townland, with a 'tablestone' (capstone) nearly 12ft in length placed over seven 'pillars' (uprights). The dolmen has not been excavated in recent times.

Some local people say that a second dolmen stood at one time on the shore of Tullynawood Lake, not far from the surviving monument, but it was broken up and carried away for various purposes in the nineteenth century. There is also a local tradition that King Lir's mythical palace once stood somewhere around Tullyvallan and that the Children of Lir, of the famous Celtic myth, wanting to have a last look at the scenes of their childhood, flew northward from Lough Derravaragh to Tullyvallan. Seeing Tullynawood Lake, they decided to rest there before flying on to the Sea of Moyle (the North Channel). Two streets in Keady are called Lir Gardens and Lir Street, recalling this tradition.

A local ballad by Tommy O'Reilly also recalls this connection:

"Twas a long weary flight from Dervarragh to Moyle
Though the foul spell impelled them, 'twas more than they could
And Finola decided they'd take an earned rest,
On the waters of fair Tullinawood.'

Sources: Bell J., *The Newry Magazine* 2, 1816, 235; Keating J., *Journal of Keady and District Historical Society*, 1992, 67-8.

❺ BALLYKEEL DOLMEN

MONUMENT TYPE	Portal Tomb with Long Cairn and Cist
LOCATION	Near Mullaghbane
GRID REFERENCE	H9950 2132
MONUMENT NUMBER	26:15
STATUS	State Care DOENI (EHS)

Ballykeel – *Baile Caol*, the narrow farmstead – is a small river valley at the western foot of Slieve Gullion Mountain. Ballykeel Dolmen, a well-preserved Neolithic monument over 5,000 years old, stands on the edge of a level terrace overlooking a tributary of the Forkill River and is known locally as 'The Hag's Chair'.

The tomb is of the tripod form, with two upright portal stones and one backstone supporting the large capstone, similar to Legananny Dolmen in Co Down. In the past portal tombs were often covered by stone cairns or earthen mounds. Very few of these survive, but at Ballykeel the remains of a stone cairn are found in association with the tomb. The dolmen is sited at the southern end of the cairn which is 0.75m high, 28.5m long and 9m wide. In 1963 Ballykeel Dolmen was excavated and the stone tomb, which had partly collapsed, was restored to its present condition, with the supporting closing slab pulled into place, the split backstone repaired and the huge capstone reinstated.

During the excavations the remains of a stone cist at the north end of the cairn were uncovered and large quantities of sherds representing various Neolithic pottery styles were found. Particularly important were the fragments of three highly decorated and elegant vessels found in the dolmen chamber. Owing to the acidity of the soil, no traces of bone survived, but analysis of earth from the chamber revealed a high phosphate content – this led the excavator to suggest that burials had originally been deposited in the tomb. Only a few pieces of worked flint were recovered, most of them finished

The restored tripod dolmen at Ballykeel

implements, including a fine javelin head, found in the cist.

Writing about Ballykeel in his last letter on 3 April 1850 to the Belfast Gaelic scholar, Robert McAdam, local poet and scribe Art Bennett said: 'There is more Irish history in the rocks of Ballykeel than ever there was possessed in Belfast. It was cradled and nursed there and more than likely will never waken'. For thousands of years this fine monument has been an element in the area's rich heritage and folklore, its ancient stones inspiring local tales of fairies, witches and hags.

Sources: Collins A.E.P., *UJA* 28, 1965, 47-70; *Creggan Journal*, 1997-8, 131.

6 CARNAVANAGHAN PASSAGE TOMB

MONUMENT TYPE	Passage Tomb
LOCATION	On a high drumlin hill west of Markethill
GRID REFERENCE	H9141 3974
MONUMENT NUMBER	16:28
STATUS	Scheduled Historic Monument

Located on the highest point of a complex drumlin hill, 6km west of Markethill, is Carnavanaghan Passage Tomb, long recognised as an important landmark in the area. From the Ordnance Survey trigonometry point now mounted on the top of the cairn, there are spectacular views over the Fews Mountains and Slieve Gullion to the south, and Armagh City to the north. It is known locally as 'The Vicar's Cairn' and it is thought that the name is derived from a local interpretation of the townland name, *Carn na Mhanaghan* – the monks' cairn.

The cairn, which is over 4,500 years old, is roughly circular and measures 32m in diameter, standing over 4m high above the ground surface at the south. Like many other stone monuments it has been robbed of stone at the north end where much of the cairn has been

'The Vicar's Cairn'

removed. In an article written in 1819, James Stuart, an historian, polemic and poet who was editor of *The Newry Telegraph* (1816–19) and *The Belfast Newsletter* (1821–54), describes the removal of 'an enormous mass of stone' from the site under the direction of Messrs Bell and Henderson in 1816. Bell, a local landlord living at Killevy Castle, had an interest in archaeology and 'led' digs in many of the areas best-known sites. The excavation notes report that nothing 'worthy of notice' was found except 'a sewer which had formed along the bottom of the tumulus'.

This account of the early excavation suggests that the cairn covers a Neolithic passage tomb similar to those found at Loughcrew and in the Bend of the Boyne, Co Meath. Other early accounts relate the discovery of a passage or chamber in 1789, and in 1797 describe the monument as a conical mound of stones surrounded by a kerb of stone about 0.75m in height. In 1802 a series of rectangular marks was noted on one of the kerb stones and John Bell, who excavated the site in 1816, describes the kerb as consisting of fifty five stones 'in an imperfect condition'. On one of the stones he noted the 'almost obliterated trace of seven concentric circles, nicely carved in regular grooves'. These two references may suggest that 'The Vicar's Cairn' was once decorated with elaborate passage-tomb art, but no examples of it can now be seen at the site.

It is said that Mr Bell enticed local people to help open the cairn in 1816 by claiming that he had found silver coins at the site. Stuart wrote in one of his letters dated 1819: 'hence many of them were induced to work with eagerness in the hopes of finding treasure. Others however who entertained a high veneration for this ancient monument replaced at night the stones which the stronger party had removed in the course of the day and thus, for a long time retarded the work'.

Sources: *PSAMNI*, 1940, 70; Bell, J., *The Newry Magazine* 2, 1816.

⑦ SLIEVE GULLION SOUTH CAIRN

MONUMENT TYPE	Passage Tomb
LOCATION	On the southern summit of Slieve Gullion
GRID REFERENCE	J0246 2032
MONUMENT NUMBER	28:07
STATUS	State Care DOENI (EHS)

Slieve Gullion – *Sliabh gCullinn*, the mountain of the steep slope – is the highest mountain in Co Armagh, the centre of a volcanic ring-dyke complex unique in Northern Ireland. On the southern summit of Slieve Gullion is a large stone cairn which covers a Neolithic passage tomb, similar in plan form to Newgrange, and known locally as the 'Calliagh Berra's House'. Located at a height of 573m, it is believed to be the highest surviving passage tomb in Ireland and on a clear day the views are magnificent. North of the cairn is a small lake, known as the 'Calliagh Berra's Lough', reputed to be bottomless. The Calliagh Berra, the hag or witch of Beara (Co

Finn Mac Cool and the 'Calliagh Berra's Lough'

Cork), is a common character in Irish folklore, often associated with passage tombs and cairns, eg at Loughcrew, Co Meath, where we find 'The Hag's Chair' and the low mountain, *Sliabh na Calliagh*.

The circular cairn is 30m in diameter and stands over 4m high above the peaty heather banks. It has a retaining kerb of large granite stones and is built, using mainly local stone, to cover an octagonal chamber which is reached along a short passage, 4.5m long. The passage is roofed with stone lintels, and the central chamber, although now partly collapsed, shows very fine stone corbelling similar to that at Newgrange. The earliest written reference to the passage tomb is found in a letter dated 1739, and in 1788 Charlotte Brooke, the

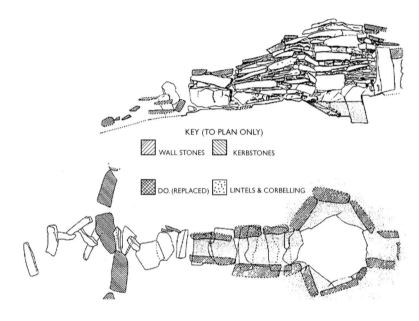

KEY (TO PLAN ONLY)

WALL STONES   KERBSTONES

DO. (REPLACED)   LINTELS & CORBELLING

Plan of Passage Tomb, Slieve Gullion – after Collins and Wilson, 1963

author of a book entitled *Reliques of Irish Poetry* (1789), recorded an
account of the opening of a chamber by local people who were looking
for the 'Calliagh Berra'. Nothing was found apart from fragments of
bone and charcoal.

During excavations in 1961 it was discovered that the burial
deposits had been badly disturbed by treasure-seekers, but tiny
fragments of cremated bone and a few worked flints were found. The
excavators also unearthed many interesting structural features and
three roughly hollowed basins believed to have been used for burial
deposits, one of which was removed to Armagh Museum. Close
examination of the stones in the tomb did not reveal any passage
tomb-art, which may be explained by the hard nature of the granite. A
bulge on the cairn's north side is probably the remains of a small cairn.

No finds were recovered, but it may date from the Bronze Age.

A second cairn, which is believed to date from the Bronze Age, (2000BC–500BC), is on the northern summit of Slieve Gullion. It measures 13.5m in diameter and stands just over 1m high. A foxhole dug into the centre of the cairn by American soldiers training in the area during the Second World War disturbed the cairn, and this may explain why no central burial cist was found when the site was excavated in 1961. Of the two cists which were found in the cairn, one held remains of burnt bone and fragments of food-vessel pottery.

A local folk tale tells of Finn McCool's adventures on the mountain and the loss of his flowing locks of blond hair:

> Sure they say, the oul' people of long ago, that Finn was going up the mountain by the lake and he saw a lady sittin' looking sad and sorrowful. He inquired as to her dilemma and she told him she had lost her ring into the lake. He assures her he would get it and jumps in. He appears some time later with the ring but the minute he steps out of the lake on to land he turns into an old withered man with hair as white as snow. The woman was Calliagh Berra and she had put a spell on Finn. Well, eventually they got him back to himself but his hair stayed white and don't you or nobody ever swim in that lake on top of Slieve Gullion or your hair will turn white ... didn't I see it happen myself!

Slieve Gullion remains a magical place, perhaps because it has attracted people to its summit for over 4,500 years. The magic and mystery of the passage tomb has inspired folk tales and stories which have helped it survive, unlike many other cairns and stone monuments. It has remained an important landmark in the landscape, standing proud above the peaty surface of the mountain, and still commands extensive views over south Ulster, north Leinster and beyond. Just remember not to swim in the lake!

Sources: Paterson T.G.F., 1945, 31-2 and 49-50; Collins, A.E.P. and Wilson B.C.S, *UJA* 26, 1963, 19-40; Murphy, M.J., *Now You're Talking* ..., 1975,101-3.

⑧ MULLYARD STANDING STONE, DERRYNOOSE

MONUMENT TYPE	Megalith/ Standing Stone
LOCATION	Mullyard, near Derrynoose
GRID REFERENCE	H7991 3110
MONUMENT NUMBER	19:12
STATUS	Recorded Historic Monument

Derrynoose – *Daoire Núis,* the oakwood of the stag – is a small hamlet west of Keady on the border with Co Monaghan. The standing stone is situated on the highest point of a drumlin hill with panoramic views all around. It has been incorporated into a stone field boundary and stands about 2m high. If you place yourself with your back to the

Three thieves turn to stone as they escape
over Mullyard Mountain

stone you can feast your eyes on what local people will tell you is one of the finest views in Ireland. Stretched before you lie the counties of Armagh and Tyrone and the Sperrin Mountains to the north, a large part of Monaghan and Cavan to the west and to the northeast Lough Neagh.

A second standing stone was once sited on the east side of the bank, but there is no longer any trace of it, sadly a situation all too common with archaeological monuments. It was, however, noted during the 1960s that the field bank was stonier around the standing stone than elsewhere, suggesting that the surviving stone may be the last remnants of a destroyed megalithic tomb.

Tradition says that long ago three thieves stole the sacred vessels from Derrynoose old church (in Listarkelt) and, as they escaped over Mullyard Mountain they were turned to stone! Three standing stones, representing the thieves, are said to have stood on this site.

Sources: *PSAMI,* 1940, 71; Keating, J., *Journal of Keady and District Historical Society,*1992, 70-1.

9 THE KING'S STABLES

MONUMENT TYPE	Earthwork
LOCATION	1km west of Navan Fort
GRID REFERENCE	H8388 4546
MONUMENT NUMBER	12:14
STATUS	State Care DOENI (EHS)

The area around Navan Fort appears to have been a very special landscape in the Late Bronze Age and the Iron Age, over 2,000 years ago. Located in a low-lying inter-drumlin hollow about 1km west of Navan Fort is the site known as 'The King's Stables'. This unusual monument is a deep man-made pool and it lies at the foot of a hill on which the large hilltop enclosure called 'Haughey's Fort' stands.

The pool, which is now heavily overgrown, measures 30m across

'The King's Stables'

and is about 2m to 3m deep . It is enclosed by a low penannular bank which is now planted with trees. A small trial excavation, directed by Dr Chris Lynn in 1975, revealed some very interesting information about the origin and function of the site. The excavation showed that the pool was a man-made feature dating from the Late Bronze Age and contemporary with the activity of that era at Navan. Clay moulds used for making bronze swords were found at the edges of the pool and many bones from red deer, dogs, cattle, sheep and pigs were retrieved from the bottom. These appear to have been deposited as part of a ritual, and even more sinister was the discovery of the facial part of a human skull at the bottom of the pool.

The excavator concluded that The King's Stables was a 'ritual lake', the centre of some sort of water cult, a role taken over by Loughnashade at a later period. Although the excavation did not unearth the bones of any dragon, folklorist George Paterson collected a story about a dragon who guards the pool:

Pearls and gold galore lie in the lake but the divil a one has ever seen them, for the dragon won't let a body near them, who has not the rightful blood of the owner in him. It has been seen twice in recent years by oul' O'Rourke. It give him such a fright he never went back to the lake. But he was not the last to see it, for sure you know there's a passage from it to the King's Stables beyond. And one day over in Tray – you know the place – it's always full with water and there the Kings of Ulster in the oul' days watered their horses and washed their chariots, like. Well, the bold O'Toole thought he would drain the water away, and he started to cut the bank and it so lovely and round it was a pity to destroy the shape. But it was little diggin' he did for up popped the dragon, spittin' something and its awful eyeballs wicked with fire. O'Toole took off – and sure he's not the same man since.

Ritual sites like The King's Stables are rare. They reveal a deep-rooted attachment to a water cult, in which ritual deposits have been amassed. Although the pool may no longer look very impressive, it

'Up popped the dragon, spittin' something and its awful eyeballs wicked with fire'

is a site of strong atmosphere, and it certainly had a clearly defined role in Bronze Age society. Who knows what mysteries the dragon protects beneath those murky waters?

Sources: Paterson T.G.F., 1945, 45-6; Lynn C.J., *UJA 30,* 1977, 42-62.

⑩ THE DANE'S CAST

MONUMENT TYPE	Linear Earthwork, visible at several points
LOCATION	Just northwest of Meigh village
GRID REFERENCE	J048 226 – J055 210
MONUMENT NUMBER	29:16
STATUS	Scheduled Historic Monument

Although little remains of this once extensive linear earthwork, commonly known as 'The Dane's Cast', it appears to have consisted of a ditch with a bank on the downslope side. Patchy remnants can be

An aerial view of 'The Dane's Cast' at Aghayalloge

traced along a 2km section, from the south end of Camlough, in the vicinity of Ballinliss School, curving to the northeast and then fading out in the townland of Aghayalloge, southeast of the main Newry to Meigh road.

The best-preserved section of the earthwork can be traced for a length of 60m across a hillslope in a field in Aghayalloge. Now used as a field boundary, the 'Cast' measures about 15m wide and consists of a rough stone wall on the east side, a ditch 3m to 4m wide and an earthen bank 1m high and about 5m to 6m wide. The wall is not an original feature but was added to reinforce the upper edge or lip of the ditch.

Linear earthworks known as 'The Dane's Cast' are also found in other parts of the county, including at Killycapple and Killyfaddy. A length in Killeen, near Armagh City, now disappeared, was known locally as 'The Rampar' and local folklore relates tales of woe concerning those who interfere with 'The Dane's Cast':

> The Killeen 'Rampar' is a gentle place. There wur lots of wee people on it in days past. I cud show ye a house near it that had to be rebuilt. It wus first put on the 'Rampar', but every night something happened to what wus built during the day. So it had to be moved. A man of the wee people rode the 'Rampar' on horseback in them days. He wus a wee man on a wee wee white pony horse, an' he wus king of them all ...

In Killyfaddy townland the entrenchment is called locally 'The Hog's Back' and is reputed to be haunted by a ghostly pig. At one time people were afraid to cross it after dark, and in the old days little bags of oatmeal were attached to necklets and hung around children's necks to keep the fairies away, as it was believed that otherwise the fairies would steal the children.

Sources: *PSAMNI*, 1940, 70 and 78; Paterson T.G.F., 1945, 78-81.

⓫ THE DORSEY

MONUMENT TYPE	Linear Earthwork
LOCATION	Southeast of Cullyhanna
GRID REFERENCE	H936 190 – J955 197
MONUMENT NUMBER	28:08
STATUS	Scheduled Historic Monument

The Dorsey – *Na Doirse*, the gateways – is an extensive earthwork which runs through the south Armagh area. The Dorsey Ramparts, or 'The Walls' as they are known locally, are said to have been a fortified frontier post to the kingdom whose capital was *Emain Macha* (Navan Fort), blocking an important historic route into south Armagh. It was built at a time when the power of the Ulster kingdom may have been at its strongest, around 100BC. Some time later Ulster was threatened from the south and it is thought that The Dorsey may have been incorporated into a more extensive defensive system known in

The Dorsey, with the Cloghfhin, or White Stone of Watching, in the foreground.

Monaghan and further west as 'The Black Pig's Dyke'.

The Dorsey is one of the few monuments in the north which have been confirmed as Iron Age in date. It is a group of linear earthworks with a perimeter of 4km, enclosing an area of 300 acres. Field survey and excavation have shown that The Dorsey included the following elements: on the south side are two separate sections of massive dykes consisting of a bank between two large ditches, with traces of another bank on the south side; on the north side the earthwork is a single bank and ditch, broken in parts and not as massive as on the south; on the east a large bank and ditch run parallel to the Ummeracam River; while on the west side a ditch and wooden palisade (revealed in excavation) flanked the bog.

Analysis of timber from a palisade and piling in the southwestern boggy area has produced a dating of around 95 BC, the same period as the timber used in the 40m structure at Navan Fort. This has led some archaeologists to suggest a cultural link between the two sites, implying that The Dorsey controlled access to *Emain Macha*. The earthworks are strategically located on the southern approaches to the Fews Mountains, across a low-lying gap and ancient route into north Armagh.

Although it has sometimes been described as an enclosure, archaeologist Dr Chris Lynn has persuasively argued that The Dorsey probably evolved through more than one phase of construction and was deliberately situated at the focal point of several routes. He also suggested that the site name, meaning 'the doors' or 'gates', indicates that the earthworks may have controlled access, rather than barring it altogether. A standing stone close to The Dorsey, in Tullynavall townland, is called the Cloghfin, or 'Calliagh Berra's Stone', or the 'White Stone of Watching'

. It features in a story about the 'Mass bush' at Dorsey, a place where Mass would have been celebrated in secret during Penal times:

> A gentle thorn sheltered the altar and there was great anger about the cuttin' of it. He who owned the land in the old days wouldn't have had it happened no matter what he was offered. He would really have been annoyed. He was a Carragher and he whitewashed the White Stone each year in the spring, but he's gone now and since he died it gets no whitewash.

This important monument can now be seen, in places neglected and overgrown, at various points along its course. The famed fortified frontier of Ulster is now virtually unknown and hardly recognisable as a major monument, but once you are inside its massive earthen ditches the significance it had in the history of Ulster soon becomes clear.

Sources: Paterson, T.G.F., 1945, 95; *Emania* 6, 1989.

⑫ NAVAN FORT

MONUMENT TYPE	Complex Earthwork
LOCATION	West of Armagh City
GRID REFERENCE	H847 452
MONUMENT NUMBER	12:15
STATUS	State Care DOENI (EHS)

Navan Fort can be confidently identified as *Emain Macha* – of heroic literature, chief residence of the kings of Ulster, and, according to tradition, destroyed in AD332. It is also one of the most important archaeological sites in Ireland. The earthworks occupy a low drumlin and command extensive views in all directions. The encircling earthwork consists of a large ditch with an external bank enclosing an area of 12 acres. Excavation across the ditch in 1998 established that

'Site B' on Navan Fort in autumn

it dates from the Iron Age, the same period as the structure on the hilltop within the enclosure.

Between 1961 and 1971 Dudley Waterman investigated two sites in the enclosure. Site A is visible as a circular earthwork with a low external bank around an inner ditch. Excavation showed that the ditch cut through circular wooden structures, datable to the Iron Age, and the earthwork can best be interpreted as a ring-barrow of later in the Iron Age.

Site B is a prominent mound measuring 50m in diameter and 6m high (reconstructed after excavation). Excavation has revealed evidence of occupation from the Neolithic period onwards, although not continuously. In the Late Bronze Age a circular ditched enclosure was built, with a ring of posts inside it. Much later, in the Iron Age, the interior was occupied by a series of circular enclosures, smaller ones joined to larger enclosures. These structures/houses were rebuilt many times. Finds included bronze and iron objects but, most remarkably, the skull of a Barbary ape. How this exotic creature found its way to Armagh is a matter for speculation!

In about 100BC, the round 'houses' were cleared away and a massive circular structure, measuring 40m across, was built. It was composed of four major concentric rings of posts within an outer post-ring (wall) and around a large central post. The structure was later filled with limestone blocks, burned, and then sealed with a mound of sods and clay. The central post has been dated by dendrochronology (tree rings) to 95BC, about the same date as the felling of the timber from The Dorsey palisade (11).

Lying northeast of the Navan enclosure is Loughnashade, natural in origin and once a substantially larger lake than at present. In 1798 four large bronze horns or trumpets were found at the edge of the lake, together with 'human skulls and other bones'. These finds must have been ritually deposited, probably by the inhabitants of Navan Fort. Only one of the horns survives, known as the Loughnashade trumpet, and it is in the National Museum in Dublin.

Scholars believe that *Emain Macha* may have been known by Ptolemy, a Greek astronomer in the second century AD, who recorded many Irish landmarks in his map, including the Boyne and the Shannon rivers. Its importance must have influenced the establishment of a very early church nearby at *Ard Macha*, by the late seventh century claimed as a foundation of St Patrick. In 1005 King Brian Boru camped at Navan Fort; the Ulster king, Niall O'Neill built a house there in 1387 and, according to law, the High King of Ireland was expected to be received and feasted at *Emain Macha* as he travelled around Ireland. One source states that it was believed that any Ulsterman who did not visit *Emain Macha* on Hallowe'en would be driven mad and die the next day!

The important body of early Irish legends known as the Ulster Cycle centres round King Conchobar (Conor) who ruled his kingdom from *Emain Macha*. It is said that there were three great halls there; one for the kings, one for the severed heads and spoils of war and another for the javelins, shields and swords. Conor's hall had 150 inner rooms and 'the walls were made of red yew with copper rivets'. It is also said that Conor never sat down to eat without 150 men around him. As well as the Red Branch Knights (*Creabruad*) there was a boy troop of 150 who were fostered at the royal site and trained and exercised on the playing field east of *Emain Macha,* and it was here that the young *Cú Chulainn* came to take on and single-handedly defeat the boy troop in a game of hurling.

East of Navan is a large, water-filled quarry hole and an industrial site. In 1985 there was a long public inquiry into an application to extend the quarry around the fort, but this was refused. Much activity followed this decision, including the setting up of the Navan Research Group, which publishes a journal, *Emania,* and the opening of the Navan Centre, southwest of the fort, which tells the story of *Emain Macha* and the excavations.

Sources: *Emania* 1.1986; Hynes, J. and Campbell, M., *Armagh City of Light and Learning*, Cottage Publications, 1997; Waterman D.M. (ed Lynn C.J.), *Excavations at Navan Fort 1961-71*, Belfast, 1997.

⓭ CORLISS FORT

MONUMENT TYPE	Bivallate Rath and Souterrain
LOCATION	Northwest of Crossmaglen
GRID REFERENCE	H8913 1667
MONUMENT NUMBER	30:01
STATUS	Scheduled Historic Monument

Corliss Fort has been described as one of the best-preserved bivallate raths in Co Armagh. Raths, or ringforts as they are commonly known, are enclosed farmsteads of the Early Christian period and are the most common monument type in Ireland. Corliss Fort is a large rath with two surrounding banks (bivallate) and an intervening ditch. It commands fine views across the drumlin landscape west of Crossmaglen. The fort is situated on the summit of a small hillock in an area of rocky scrubland, and is now surrounded by mature beech trees, overlooking a crannog in Lough Ross and two other forts in the townlands of Tullyard and Lisamry. The earthwork is known locally as 'The Beech Fort' or 'Donaghy's Fort'.

The interior of this rath is rather square in shape, measuring 40m by 39m and sloping gently to the north. The surface of the interior is quite uneven and in the centre is the entrance to an L-shaped souterrain, built of drystone-walling.

Two well-defined banks surround the fort. The inner bank is still upstanding in substantial lengths to a height of around 1.5m and it falls to an impressive deep U-shaped ditch, around 6m-7m deep. The outer bank stands about 3m above the ditch and the exterior face has been strengthened in parts with drystone walls.

There are two exceptionally well-defined entrances to the rath and it is thought that a local landowner may have modified them in the nineteenth century. He was also responsible for planting the beech trees around the external bank of the rath, presumably to enhance the appearance of the site.

The rath was excavated in 1939 and, while little in the way of settlement debris was recovered apart from a few pieces of bone and

Corliss Fort, showing the intervening ditch

sherds, postholes were found on the outer edge of the inner bank.
Measuring 0.5m in depth and width, they led the excavator to
postulate that they were the remains of a timber palisade. Happily,
Corliss Fort has survived the ravages of modern agriculture and
remains a very fine example of an Early Christian farmstead,
providing a window into the agricultural communities of the area in
the first millennium AD. The timber palisade which once surrounded
the fort may indicate a need to defend one's home and possessions at
that time, and although ringforts became a standard settlement type
from around AD600, it is thought locally that Corliss Fort was lived
in until the seventeenth century.

Sources: Davies O., *CLAJ* 9, 1940, 338-43.

⑭ LISLEITRIM FORT

MONUMENT TYPE	Multivallate Rath
LOCATION	Southwest of Cullyhanna village
GRID REFERENCE	J9035 2072
MONUMENT NUMBER	27:03
STATUS	Scheduled Historic Monument

Aerial view of Lisleitrim Fort, showing the three surrounding banks

Lisleitrim – *Lios laith droma*, the grey fort of the ridge – is a hilly townland in the drumlin landscape of southeast Ulster. On an exposed hilltop west of Cullyhanna is Lisleitrim Fort, a fine example of a multivallate rath (a rath with several banks and ditches). It overlooks a crannog in Lisleitrim Lough in the valley below and has been described as one of the most spectacular multivallate raths in the county, known locally as 'the hero's important fort'.

The interior of the rath, which is roughly oval, measures 41m by 49m and slopes gently to the south. John Donaldson, an ordnance surveyor who worked in the area, noted in 1838 'a cave (souterrain)

in the centre which is now closed up'. The interior is defined around its perimeter by a steep scarp that falls to a ditch nearly 7m wide. Beyond this are two banks and ditches, on a large scale of almost 6m wide and 2m deep, and an outer or third bank which has been incorporated into a field boundary. There are some doubts as to whether this bank is original, although Donaldson recounts that the site was enclosed by 'three ramparts' (banks) in 1838. A mound of earth at the north side is debris from amateur excavations carried out in the 1960s.

The proximity of the site to Lisleitrim crannog has prompted the suggestion that this may have been a royal rath, since there are other examples of this juxtaposition at royal sites. Donaldson reported that a type of cooking spit and iron pot were discovered in the crannog, while a small trial excavation in 1966 produced finds of pottery and layers of ash and charcoal. The local people say the banshee was often heard screeching at the edge of the waters around Lisleitrim crannog and a famous local tale tells how a spirit came to a nearby house:

> My father's house has a spirit in it to this very day. Many a time I heard the footsteps. This is how it came about. Burnett who was a Precentor in Freeduff (a Presbyterian Meeting House in Creggan Parish), was a just and righteous man, but he fell behind with his rent and had to give up his farm, and to please the landlord we had to take it and add it to our own … and to cut a long story short, Burnett took the leaving of the place so much to heart, he went down on his bare knees and prayed prayers upon us that have certainly come to pass – for there is no longer one of our name in it, and indeed it's nothing but troubles we had while there. And if you ask me what the restless spirit in the house is I can only say that I am sure it is Burnett. His prayers were answered. God in his wisdom chose to punish him by sending him back to stay at the house he cursed until Judgement Day and that's that!

While raths are common in the landscape of Ireland, very fine multivallate raths like Lisleitrim are rare and an important reminder of the country's early social hierarchy. High-status raths are thought to have acted as focal points for smaller sites, and it has been suggested that they belonged to the royal and major 'land-owning' elite of Early Christian Ireland.

Sources: Donaldson J., 1923, 51; Paterson T.G.F., 1945, 21-2; Aalen F.H.A., Whelan K., Stout M., *Atlas of the Irish Rural Landscape*, Cork, 1997, 44-9.

⑮ RATHTRILLICK

MONUMENT TYPE	Multivallate rath
LOCATION	South of Middletown
GRID REFERENCE	H7575 3795
MONUMENT NUMBER	15:20
STATUS	Scheduled
Historic Monument	

Rathtrillick — *Ráth na Trileac,* the rath of three (flag) stones — is an impressively sited ringfort located on the summit of a prominent drumlin overlooking the village of Middletown, close to the border with Co Monaghan. The interior of the site survives as a slightly hollowed, pentagonal platform, measuring 46m in diameter at its widest point. Along the north and west sides of the interior there are traces of a perimeter bank which stands 1m high above the interior at the northeast and is 6.5m wide, although it is not clear whether this length is original.

Aerial view of the multivallate ringfort structure

The surrounding ramparts and ditches are impressive and well preserved, although they are somewhat overgrown with trees and bushes. The inner ditch is 2.5m deep below the interior and 6.5m wide. The inner bank is particularly impressive, standing 2.75m high above the first ditch, 10m wide and 4.75m high above a second ditch which measures 6.5m in width. The outer bank is slightly less massive, standing 2m above the ditch, 8m wide and 1.5m above the field surface.

The entrance on the southeast side survives as a gap through the banks and a ramped area over the ditches. There is no trace of the souterrain, which is reputed to be located somewhere in the east side of the rath. This may have been a royal site in the Early Christian period, but it is traditionally held that it was the seat of the O'Neills who held land in the district until the rebellion of 1641. Traces of spade ridges indicate cultivation of the interior in the past, and the folklorist George Paterson recorded a story about the cultivation of flax in the fort:

> Rathtrillick fort was laboured once. That was a long time ago. An' flax wus sowed in it. Nobody thought it wud thrive, but it did. An' it wus the purtiest flax ye iver saw. But shure the night before the mornin' it was to be pulled it vanished right off the fort an' wus niver seen more. An' the seed wus lost, an' the labour wus lost. An' him that owned it nearly lost his head. The wee people were heard dancing and holding races, and the old people heard music and the horses' hooves as they flew around the ring.

Like Lisleitrim Fort (14), near Cullyhanna, Rathtrillick represents what could be described as a royal site and, with its heavily defensive banks and ditches, it made for a safe home. It was preserved by Bishop Stearn when he acquired the land in 1730, and stories of fairies and spells kept it from being developed. Although difficult to access, Rathtrillick is an important monument worthy of greater notice and respect.

Sources: *PSAMNI*, 1940, 69; Paterson, 1945, 63; *Historical Sketches of Tynan and Middletown*, ed. Mallon S., 1995,10.

⑯ THE RELIG, CASHEL HILL

MONUMENT TYPE	Cashel
LOCATION	South of Seaghan Reservoir
GRID REFERENCE	H9036 3665
MONUMENT NUMBER	28:11
STATUS	Scheduled Historic Monument

The windswept cashel on Cashel Hill

The cashel – an early circular farmstead which used stones instead of earth for its defensive wall – is located just south of the summit of Cashel Hill and commands excellent views over Seaghan Dam and the surrounding countryside. This townland in the parish of Lisnadill must derive its name from this fine monument, which is known locally as 'The Relig'.

The circular enclosure, measuring 40m in diameter, has been tilled for many years. The cashel wall is tumbled and stands 0.5m high above the interior. The wall is nearly 3m wide, but stone has been robbed from it to build modern field walls. A large stone lying on the cashel wall at the northeast is said to have marked the grave of an 'ancient king', or the burial place of a giant killed by Finn McCool.

The term 'Relig' is commonly used in Ireland to denote a graveyard or burial place, therefore we can probably safely conclude that this is so at Cashel Hill. Two possible origins for the site have been put forward, and the first is that it was a small ecclesiastical settlement in antiquity, re-used in more recent years for unconsecrated burials. The Rev Dean Reeves, writing in 1879, included the site in his notes on ancient churches in the county. The second possibility is that the cashel was non-religious in origin and was only used in recent years for burials. Folklorist George Paterson, who recorded the name 'The Relig', reported that it was used 'in days not long since' for the burial of stillborn infants. He also reported that a souterrain was present in the cashel, describing it as having chambers and four entrances. It is now closed up.

Cultivation ridges are visible inside the cashel and they inspired a folk tale, which was published by George Paterson in 1945, called The Ploughing of the Relig at Cashel:

> It was in old McParland's time it was done and the countryside was afraid for the man that done it but nothing happened. And he had the finest corn you ever saw. The heads were as long as your arm, reaching far above the wall of the Relig. When it ripened he decided to cut it. In the morning of the cutting when they all gathered to give a hand, all they found was bare land, no corn, not even a stubble. It give them such a fright they never did it again …

Another tale recorded by Paterson, entitled The Fairies and Fionn, attempts to explain the large stone in the northeast of the cashel:

> I heard me grandfather say that many a night when he would be bringing home the cattle he would have to get on the ditch in this very loanin' to let them pass on their way to the glen. There were giants here as well as the wee people. Finn McCool spent many a day on Cashel Hill. It was here he put an end to an impudent foreign giant that was looking for fighting. He is buried under the stone.

Cashel Hill is a wild and wonderful location which seems to have had an eventful past, witnessing encounters with both giants and fairies, as well as ancient kings and stone-robbers. It is said that the 'largest amber bead ever found in Ireland was discovered here', although we have no trace of it now, so perhaps this dishevelled stone cashel which crowns Cashel Hill was once acquainted with the wealthy warriors and kings which folklore records.

Sources: *PSAMNI*, 1940, 71; Paterson, 1945, 82 and 93-4; Jefferies H.A., *Seanchas Ard Mhacha* 17, 1996-7, 194-7.

⑰ KILNASAGGART PILLAR STONE

MONUMENT TYPE	Inscribed Pillar Stone and Graveyard
LOCATION	South of Jonesborough village
GRID REFERENCE	J0619 1490
MONUMENT NUMBER	32:06
STATUS	State Care DOENI (EHS)

The southeast face of
Kilnasaggart Pillar Stone

The site of Kilnasaggart – *Cill na Sagart*, the Church of the Priest – is located in a valley floor which is thought to be part of the legendary Gap of the North. It was located on one of Ireland's five great main roads, the *Slighe Midhluachra*, which ran from Tara through the Moyry Pass to Dunseverick in north Antrim.

The tall pillar stone, which now stands in a small hedged enclosure of modern date, was mentioned in a letter by ordnance surveyor John O'Donovan, writing in 1835. He records the local belief that 'a crock of gold was buried at its foot' and he feared it would be damaged by treasure-seekers. Indeed, it was overturned soon after his letter was written, but was reset by local people some time later. In excavations carried out in 1966 and 1968 it was revealed that an Early Christian graveyard with stone-built and dug graves, all orientated E–W, surrounds the stone. Finds were scarce and no structures were unearthed during the excavation, but a roofless church is shown here in the 1609 map by the cartographer, Bodley, and the church lands belonged to the Armagh Culdees in the early sixteenth century. The Culdees were very early anchorite monks who had a settlement at Armagh. The name Culdee is derived from the Irish *Ceile Dé*, servants of God.

The stone has ten crosses carved on its northwest side and three on the southeast side. On the southeast side between two large crosses is the unusually long inscription: IN LOC SO TANIMMARNI TERNOHC MAC CERAN BIC ER CUL PETER APSTEL, recording the dedication of the place by Ternoc, son of Ceran Bic, under the patronage of Peter the Apostle. Ternoc's death is recorded in the annals in AD714 or 716, so the stone can be dated to about AD700. Other cross-carved stones of varying sizes are located around the base of the pillar and there are parts of two crosses on the large granite slab in the middle of the enclosure. A bullaun stone or 'Wart Well' – believed to have the ability to cure warts – is located in the field to the southwest.

The whole area west of Slieve Gullion is known as *Gleann-na-Samhaisce*, The Glen of the Heifer. The heifer, who, according to legend lived in this glen, gave milk in abundance to all who came, always filling the bucket. One day a person, through greed or malice, tried to milk the cow into a sieve. The angry cow stamped her foot on the ground and then left the valley forever. The shape of a hoof can still be seen on a stone beside the pillar stone.

Local tradition relates that the monks had a mill here, giving the nearby fields names such as Kiln Field and Mill Field, and a little eminence is called 'Shelling Hill' where the process of shelling – separating the husks from the grain – was performed by winnowing before the introduction of fans to corn mills. It is, however, likely that these names survive from much more recent milling activity and have little to do with this ancient graveyard.

Sources: Reeves W., *UJA* 1, 1853, 221-5; *CLAJ* 1904, 44-9; Paterson, 1945, 39-40; Murphy M.J., *Sayings and Stories from Slieve Gullion*, 1990, 104.

⑱ TYNAN HIGH CROSSES

MONUMENT TYPE	Crosses
LOCATION	Tynan village
GRID REFERENCE	H7662 4300
MONUMENT NUMBER	11:14
STATUS	Tynan Village Cross is in State Care DOENI (EHS)
	Tynan Terrace Cross is a Scheduled Historic
	Monument

Tynan — *Tuíneán,* the place of the (man-made) watercourse — is a small estate village built snugly into a drumlin hill 6km west of Armagh City. The village is heavily associated with the Stronge family who built their house and demesne, Tynan Abbey, south of the village. The present Church of Ireland parish church stands in a prominent hilltop position in the village and appears to occupy the site of an Early Christian church associated with St Vindic. Although there are no visible traces of an early enclosure in the churchyard, there are several stone monuments and pieces of

The inscribed panel depicting the temptation of Adam and Eve on the Village Cross, Tynan

rescued stonework which date from the tenth century onwards.

The most prominent of these is the Village Cross, located outside and south of the churchyard, made up of the remains of at least two, and possibly three crosses. It was reputedly thrown down either by Cromwellian soldiers or Puritans, and it has been extensively restored and moved at various times during its eventful life. Transferred to its present position in 1960, it now consists of three pieces. The lower shaft is decorated, featuring Adam and Eve on the west side and another less clear figure on the east side. The base may belong to the shaft, but it has been suggested that it was originally part of another cross. The head is of open-ring form and is decorated with very prominent bosses, once finely ornamented. Other stones are cemented into the graveyard wall opposite the cross. They include an undecorated cross-base, the decorated ring of a cross and a fourteen-sided sundial from the seventeenth-century.

A second cross from Tynan village was moved in about 1840 to the terrace of Tynan Abbey and is now known as the Terrace Cross. In the nineteenth century it was a feature of the terrace but is now densely overshadowed by large yew trees. Two other crosses were moved to the Abbey grounds from Glenarb in Co Tyrone. Politician and local historian, Seamus Mallon, MLA, writing on the Parish of Tynan, points out that the name Tynan Abbey is misleading as the building dates back only to the eighteenth century. As for the reason for moving these crosses, it stemmed either from a desire to protect them from weathering or from vandalism, or to give the new location an air of importance. Indeed, nineteenth-century sources suggest that the moving was to safeguard neglected monuments, but it was certainly fashionable to decorate an estate with 'rescued' pieces of stonework.

Sources: Reeves W., *JRSAI* 16 (1883-4), 412-30; *PSAMNI*, 1940, 64 and 68; Roe H.M., *Seanchas Ard Mhacha* 1955,112-13; *Historical Sketches of Tynan and Middletown*, ed. Mallon S.,1995,10; Hamlin A., *From the Isles of the North*, ed. Bourke C., Belfast, 1995, 187-96.

⑲ KILLEVY CHURCHES, GRAVEYARD AND HOLY WELL

MONUMENT TYPE	Churches, Graveyard and Holy Well
LOCATION	North of Meigh village
GRID REFERENCE	J0402 2208
MONUMENT NUMBER	29:02
STATUS	State Care DOENI (EHS)

Killevy graveyard, where, according to tradition, St Moninna is buried

The graveyard at Killevy – *Cill Sleibhe*, the Church of the Mountain – is beautifully sited on the eastern slopes of Slieve Gullion overlooking the flat plains of Meigh and the ring dyke mountains – a circular intrusion caused by the collapse of a massive volcano – beyond. This is the site of one of Ireland's most important early convents founded in the sixth century by St Moninna (from which comes the local name, Bline), also known as Darerca, 'daughter of Erc'. According to the annals, she died in AD517 or 519 and her feast day was 6 July.

Later stories tell how she built a wooden church close to Carlingford Lough and lived a strict and austere life. The site was raided by Vikings between AD795 and 830 and again in AD923. In the Middle Ages the convent was re-established as a house of Augustinian canonesses and it continued thus until it was dissolved in 1542.

The two churches are aligned east to west, but although linked by later walling, they date from different periods. The west church is the earlier, and the oldest surviving church in Co Armagh, with the west wall and its magnificent lintelled door dating from the tenth century and the rest of the structure from the twelfth. An area of stone at the southwest angle is sometimes claimed to be the base of the round tower which is known to have been blown down in about 1768. Labhrás Bacach Ó Ceallach, Redmond O'Hanlon's harper, wrote an Irish elegy for the round tower, translated as:

> O steeple of Killevy
> My grief to have thee down.
> If the two Redmonds were living,
> Thy top would not be broken.

The O'Hanlons were the displaced chieftains of the Barony of Orior. Redmond O'Hanlon was a renowned tory, – tóraidhe, robber – and rapparee – rapaire, a catpurse or bandit – who was hanged for his anti-establishment activities.

It is uncertain whether the round tower was freestanding or attached to the church.

The east church probably dates from the fifteenth century and was certainly the church for the Augustinian community. The door leading north from near the east end of the north wall may well have led to a cloister, now completely disappeared. The east window is a rare east-Ulster example of a formerly traceried window with decoration of carved heads and foliage outside.

It was known from nineteenth-century sources that a souterrain (cave) existed near the graveyard and this was recently rediscovered during the laying of water pipes. The structure was recorded, sealed and then reburied, for safety and to preserve its secret.

Killevy is still a place of burial, pilgrimage and veneration. According to tradition, a plain granite slab in the north part of the graveyard marks St Moninna's grave. Many people visit the grave and also the holy well on the mountainside, which is a focus for veneration, especially on her feast day, 6 July. The well is reached by a path which runs along the exterior of the north wall of the graveyard and up the mountain. The spring well which is now marked by a shrine is known locally as St Bline's Well, and is reputed to have healing properties for eye ailments. The shrine, built in 1931 by Mr W Grant of Newry, shines white in the sun and can be seen from miles around, a reminder of the saint who lived here fifteen hundred years ago.

Sources: Davies O., *CLAJ* 9, 1938, 77-86; Gwynn and Hadcock 1970, 321; Ó hÓgáin, D., *Myth, Legend and Romance*, 1991, 304.

20 CHURCH AND HOLY WELL, DERRYNOOSE

MONUMENT TYPE	Church and Holy Well
LOCATION	Southwest of Keady
GRID REFERENCE	H793 322
MONUMENT NUMBER	19:10
STATUS	Recorded Historic Monument

The early church settlement at Derrynoose is associated with St Mochua, better known as the patron of Timahoe in Co Laois. He died in the middle of the seventh century, so may have founded the church at Derrynoose in the late sixth or early seventh century. Nothing else is known about Derrynoose until it emerges as a parish church in the early fourteenth century. By the early part of the seventeenth century a Protestant church had been built on the prominent hilltop, and what remains, precariously balanced, is a fragment of that church, waiting, it is said, to fall on a redheaded female of the McMahon clan!

The well of St Mochua, at the foot of the hill, has probably been the focus for pilgrimage for many centuries. The well is credited with having curative properties for eye ailments. Whilst many came to pray for the intercession of St Mochua, others came to kneel on *Leac Mochua*, the cursing stone, to call down misfortune on those they

Curative waters of St Mochua's Holy Well

felt had wronged them. Local people called this 'praying prayers on them'. Canon Kelly (1806-1891) entrusted two local men, Dan Mc Keown and Paul Haughey, with the task of removing the stone and burying it. He also elicited from them a solemn promise that they would never reveal its hiding place – and both died with the secret. The stone has never been found, but it has inspired many stories. Folklorist George Paterson recorded the following tradition about the well:

> Here between sunset and sunrise there was a cure for everything and beside the well was a wishing stone. It had to be turned at night, but there was them that wished troubles on their neighbours, so the stone is not there now. Some of the countryside who had misfortunes through it gathered one night and dug a hole both wide and deep and there it lies somewhere near, buried far beneath the clay.

Today at the side of the road from Keady to Monaghan we find a well-presented shrine built into the hillside and a tidy holy well. The well is still a location for local pilgrimage. Rags, personal belongings and statues can be found tied to trees around the well, a symbol of the continuing religious significance of Derrynoose to local people, fourteen hundred years after its foundation by St Mochua.

Sources: Paterson, 1945, 98 and 107-8; Arthurs J.B., 1954, 33-8; Keating, J., *Journal of Keady and District Historical Society*, 1992, 73-6.

21 TASSAGH GRAVEYARD

MONUMENT TYPE	Graveyard and Site of Church
LOCATION	Northwest of Tassagh Post Office
GRID REFERENCE	H8653 3771
MONUMENT NUMBER	16:51
STATUS	Recorded Historic Monument

Close to the west bank of the River Callan, the raised graveyard is enclosed by a modern stone wall. It is claimed locally that Tassagh Graveyard is the second earliest Christian cemetery in Ireland. The River Callan runs through the area and some scholars say that Tassagh takes its name from *an tEas,* – the waterfall– although it is generally accepted to be *an Tasach*, the dwelling.

Local tradition relates that there was a monastery here, but there is

Cú Chulainn watering his horse at Tassagh Bridge

no recorded early history of the site nor any definite link with St Tassach. Reputed to have lived in the fifth century, St Tassach was a craftsman and is said to have made a receptacle for the Cross of Jesus, one of the treasures of the See of Armagh. In the medieval period Tassagh was part of the Rectory of Derrynoose held by the Armagh Culdees – anchorite monks believed to be the earliest priests of God – and the graveyard was their traditional burial ground. A local story recalls the tradition of the Culdees at Tassagh:

> In a graveyard down in Tassagh
> where the holy Culdees sleep,
> Side by side both Gael and Planter
> Now a peaceful vigil keep.
> In this green and lovely valley
> By the quiet Callan side
> 'neath the same sod, long forgotten,
> vengeful Celt, and Saxon pride.

A raised circular area defined by a steep scarp and ditch at the west, southwest and northwest probably indicates an early enclosure. The surface of the platform is uneven and covered with numerous grave slabs, a few recent, but the majority much older, inscribed with rough lettering or initials. A stone decorated with a simple Latin cross is located near the southeast corner and may be medieval in date. There is now no surface evidence of a church in the graveyard, but the 1609 Escheated Counties map for the Barony of Armagh shows a church, probably roofed, at Ballintasse. From time to time early material has been found in the graveyard and its environs. According to the surveyor Samuel Lewis, an antique ring set with a large emerald was discovered at the site in 1824, and local tradition relates the discovery of a seal and sword hilt during construction of a nearby mill-race.

The site of Tassagh Bridge, a little south of the graveyard, was known as the Ford of the Watching and it is said that Cú Chulainn used to water his horses at this point, safe in the knowledge that he could observe all around him.

Sources: Lewis S., 1837, II, 34; Arthurs J.B., 1954, 38; Grangemore GAA, *Oscailt Oifigiuil Pairc Naomh Mhuire, Grainseach Mhor*, 1984, 117; Carville G., *Creggan: A Celtic Christian Site*, Dundalk, 1996, 57; Donnelly C.J., 1997, 107-108.

22 FRANCISCAN FRIARY, ARMAGH

MONUMENT TYPE	Franciscan Friary
LOCATION	The Palace Demesne, Armagh City
GRID REFERENCE	H8764 4477
MONUMENT NUMBER	12:16
STATUS	State Care DOENI (EHS)

The ruins of the Franciscan Friary are located on the southeast edge of Armagh City near the entrance to the grounds of the Palace Demesne, now the offices of Armagh City and District Council. The Friary was founded by Archbishop Patrick O'Scannail in 1263–4. In its heyday it was patronised by prominent members of Irish society and some of them are buried here, including Gormlaith O'Donnell, wife of Domhnall O'Neill, interred in 1353. The Friary was dissolved in 1542 and was burned by Shane O'Neill in 1561 and again by Hugh O'Neill in 1593, to prevent its use by English soldiers. In 1618 the site became part of the Archbishop's demesne and much stone was robbed for use elsewhere. An enclosure ditch – a protective embankment often found surrounding early Christian sites – was open until the late eighteenth century when it was removed during the landscaping of the demesne by Archbishop Robinson.

Archaeological investigation in the 1970s confirmed that the church dates largely from the thirteenth century, and at 49.8m in length, it is reputed to be the longest friary church in Ireland. During excavation over one thousand skeletons were discovered in the interior, and reburied. The west end of the church is quite well preserved, with a west door and two arches which led into a south

The ruins of the church - Franciscan Friary, Armagh

aisle, now missing, though one of the arches has been partly reconstructed. The east end of the church is more ruined, possibly arising from the collapse of the fifteenth-century tower, located at the junction of the nave and chancel. Also at the east end are two tomb recesses, two empty graves and a rare survival of a medieval altar. Almost nothing remains of the cloister, formerly north of the church, although excavation in the 1960s revealed evidence of medieval occupation near the ring road.

Sources: Gwynn and Hadcock, 1970, 242; Lynn C.J., *UJA* 38, 1975, 61-80.

㉓ MOYRY CASTLE

MONUMENT TYPE	Castle and Bawn
LOCATION	South of Jonesborough
GRID REFERENCE	J0576 1466
MONUMENT NUMBER	32:05
STATUS	State Care DOENI (EHS)

Moyry Castle – *Caisleán Bhealach an Mhaighre*, the castle of the Moyry
Pass – is prominently sited on a rock outcrop overlooking the
strategically important Moyry Pass or Gap of the North. Charles
Blount, also known as Lord Deputy Mountjoy, built the tower as a
military stronghold in June 1601. A Dutch engineer, Levan de Rose,
supervised the building of the castle and it was completed 'within the
month'. The castle was then garrisoned almost immediately by
Captain Anthony Smith and a contingent of twelve men.

Set within a bawn, only a small part of which now survives, the
three-storied tower has rounded corners, many pistol loops and a
machicolation, or 'drop hole', over the door, used to discourage

Moyry Castle and a fragment of the surrounding bawn wall

intruders from attempting to break down the door. Conditions in the castle would have been spartan, to say the least, and it is thought that longterm occupation was not planned. The fireplaces and windows were located at the first- and second-floor level, and access to the living quarters was by ladders, as there were no stairs. The machicolation and latrine were located on the wall-walk, also reached by a ladder.

The Moyry Pass has always been an important route through the mountains into the north, and it still is, with the main north-south railway line running through it. It has often been a troubled area and it has been described recently as a pass 'with a most unsavory reputation, not a pass in the usual sense of the lowest point between two mountains; it was, rather, a glen or valley, with a causeway of wooden planks, running between extensive bogs and thick woodland' (C.E.B. Brett).

Moyry Pass remained under the control of the Irish until the early seventeenth century when the castle was built. In 1343 the Justiciary, Sir Ralph Ufford, suffered not only the indignity of losing his men while attempting to navigate the pass but also 'his clothes, his money, his vessels of silver and some of his horses ...'

By the time Lord Deputy Mountjoy was in the area in the early seventeenth century, the pass was still treacherous. He was attacked by 1,200 foot and 220 horse soldiers as he tried in vain to make his way through the Gap of the North in May 1600. In 1601 Hugh O'Neill and his army, for reasons still unknown, left the pass, and Mountjoy and his men marched through the undefended Moyry Pass, clearing it of the dense woodland shown in contemporary maps as they did so. In 1603 Hugh O'Neill surrendered to Mountjoy and received a pardon from the Queen, thus securing his life and lands. After this, the Moyry Pass provided a relatively safe passage from north to south for the local chieftains and their supporters. In 1641 the confederates garrisoned the castle and between August and September of 1689 King William's army under the command of Frederick Herman, Duke of Schomberg marched from Belfast through this pass to Dundalk on their way to the Battle of the Boyne.

Folklorist George Paterson recorded a story about the Moyry Cat:

> He was here in Finn's time and for hundreds of years after ... He
> would kill men and animals alike when the temper was upon him ...
> And he ruled all the cats of Ireland and one day made a plot to put an
> end to the men of Oriel. But the secret leaked out and a party set out
> to kill or be killed by him. And the leader had a sword with a charm
> and it was he who had the luck to slice the head off him. As the head
> fell down it said to him 'when you go home tell yer kitten what you
> have done to me'. The man went home and when he told the kitten it
> lepped at him and tore his throat open and killed him.

Moyry Castle still stands, overlooking the railway line, guarding
the historic Moyry Pass four hundred years after its construction –
not bad for a castle where longterm occupation was not planned!

Sources: *PSAMNI* 1940, 79; Paterson 1945, 35-6; Hayes-McCoy
1964, 2; Brett C.E.B., *Buildings of County Armagh,* Belfast, 1999, 18-19.

24 BALLYMOYER OLD CHURCH

MONUMENT TYPE	Church and Graveyard
LOCATION	Ballintemple, 2 km southwest of Whitecross
GRID REFERENCE	H9644 3077
MONUMENT NUMBER	21:30
STATUS	Scheduled Historic Monument

In the churchyard of St Luke's Church of Ireland parish church,
Ballymoyer, are the remains of an earlier church. According to the
surveyor Samuel Lewis, the walls of the church were begun in the
reign of Charles I, but because the parson was murdered, the church
was not roofed until 1775, when Primate Robinson directed the
completion of the work. The ivy-covered church is now roofless,
heavily overgrown and in an unstable condition. It has been fenced off

for reasons of public safety. It is, however, a rare example of seventeenth-century architecture, and of particular interest are the heavy round-headed windows.

There may have been an earlier church on or near this site, but how far back it goes is not clear. Samuel Lewis, writing in 1837, claimed that 'the ancient cemetery may still be traced in the demesne of Ballymoyer Lodge', but to date this has not been substantiated, and the early history of the parish is uncertain. Some writers have confused this site with another, *Tech-talain*, mentioned in the Tripartite Life of Patrick, but recent research indicates that *Tech-talain* is

Heavy round-headed windows at Ballymoyer Old Church

Tehallan or Tyholland in Co Monaghan and not Ballymoyer.

The parish of Ballymoyer is named after the MacMoyer family who served as *maor* or keeper of the Book of Armagh. This was one of the treasures of Armagh, written in AD807, containing sources about St Patrick and other documents. The MacMoyer family was given eight townlands as payment for the safe keeping of the book.

In 1669 Oliver Plunkett was made Archbishop of Armagh and upset many of the Franciscan order by allowing the Dominicans to settle in the area. The bad blood resulted in the last hereditary keeper of the Book of Armagh, Florence MacMoyer, a Francisican friar, pawning the Book of Armagh for £5 in order to travel to London along with others to give evidence in the trial of Oliver Plunkett. Archbishop Plunkett was subsequently found guilty of treason and was hanged, drawn and quartered at Tyburn in 1680. The family never recovered the book, which was later bought by Rev William Reeves, bishop of Armagh, who was a noted historian and antiquarian and was Prebendary of Tynan (18) from 1865-75. It is now in the library of Trinity College, Dublin.

Florence MacMoyer was treated as an outcast by his people and died in 1713. He was buried in Ballymoyer graveyard where his tombstone simply read: 'Body of Florence Mac Wyre who died February 12th 1713'. The tombstone was subjected to what has been described as the 'grossest attacks' and local people left large stones on the grave and eventually covered it. A tree beside the tombstone was bound with iron hoops to prevent the evil spirit of MacMoyer getting out. It is said that the tombstone was eventually broken and was taken to Ballymoyer House. Although local people say it was used as part of the floor of an outhouse in Ballymoyer House, it has never been traced and the house has been demolished. All that remains of the once grand demesne at Ballymoyer is the tree-lined glen and avenue, now cared for by the National Trust.

Sources: Lewis 1837, I, 154-5; *CLAJ* 1906, 78-83; *PSAMNI* 1940, 72; Brett C.E.B., Belfast 1999, 11.

25 CREGGAN CHURCHYARD

MONUMENT TYPE:	Graveyard
LOCATION:	Northeast of Crossmaglen
GRID REFERENCE:	H993 158
MONUMENT NUMBER:	31:20
STATUS:	Recorded Historic Monument, Listed Building

Creggan – an *Creagán*, the rocky place – is situated near the wooded banks of the Creggan River northeast of Crossmaglen. The Church of Ireland graveyard is well known locally for containing the burial vault of the Ulster chieftain family, the O'Neills, and the graves of local eighteenth-century Gaelic poets, including Art McCooey and Patrick

Creggan Church of Ireland (1758). Note the Eastwood Vault,
left of centre – an early church?

Mac Aliondain. There are no surface remains of any great antiquity in
the graveyard and most authorities, including the late Cardinal Tomás
Ó Fiaich, consider Creggan to be a fourteenth-century foundation,
succeeding an earlier parish church nearby.

Archaeologist Dr Geraldine Carville, however, has recently argued
that one vault in the graveyard, that of the Eastwood family, is in fact
an Early Christian church, although this assertion has been strongly
contested by other archaeologists. Dr Carville maintains that certain
architectural features of the structure, including the stone roof,
buttresses, splayed window and recessed entrance, are reminiscent of
old churches like St Mochta's House in Co Louth (35), and the
churches at Glendalough in Co Wicklow. She also uses astronomical
evidence to link the church with the feast day of a local saint, St
Jarlath (Mac Trena), third Archbishop of Armagh, who died in
AD481. St Jarlath was a disciple of St Patrick and a son of a local
ruling family who, according, to Dr Carville, may have lived at
Rathtrillick (15).

The present Church of Ireland church was built in 1758 and the tower was added in 1799. It is unclear what association, if any, this structure had with the medieval church. It is possible that older work may have been incorporated into the present structure and it has been pointed out that one of the side walls in the nave is much thicker than the other, reinforcing this view. According to surveyor John Donaldson, writing in 1838, the present church foundation 'passes over, in a transverse line, and intersects at nearly right angles another ancient edifice, part of the ruins of a Roman Catholic chapel'. He goes on to say 'the O'Neills and McMahons bury their dead in a vault which it is asserted was under the altar'. This vault was rediscovered by accident in 1973 and contains numerous skulls and other bones.

During the eighteenth century, the last great age of Gaelic literature, the Ring of Gullion area played an important role in the literary history of Ulster and the area was known as *Ceanlar na nAmhrán* (The District of Songs) and *Ceanlar na bhFilí* (The District of Poets). Creggan Old Church and graveyard is the last resting place of some of these poets. Art McCooey was from Creggan and was born in 1738; his poems show his great awareness of Irish mythology and history and he was well versed in the heroes of classical literature. It is said that Art had a share of the family holding but he squandered it and spent his life as a labourer and gardener. He worked for some time for the Rector of Creggan, Rev. Hugh Hill (1728–1773), but left after the local parish priest, Fr Terence Quinn, objected. Art wished to marry his cousin, but the priest refused to marry them. Rev. Hill performed the ceremony and Fr Quinn excommunicated Art from the Catholic Church. McCooey wrote a bitter satirical poem about Fr Quinn's sister, entitled 'Blind Mary Quinn'. His most famous work is *Úr Chnoic Chéin Mhic Cáinte*, a poem set to music in praise of a young woman with whom he was in love. His work is revered and acclaimed by scholars of the Irish language. He died on 5 January 1773.

Patrick Mac Aliondain, who died in 1733, and Seamus Mór Mac Murphy, who died in 1744, are also buried in Creggan graveyard. Both were Gaelic poets and Mór Mac Murphy was also an outlaw. John Johnston, 'Johnston of the Fews', was buried in Creggan in

1759. He was the much-feared chief constable of the Fews – a mountain range which runs between Newry and Keady and thought to derive its name from Fuaith, the wood – who inspired the following couplet:

> Jesus of Nazareth, King of the Jews
> Save us from Johnston, King of the Fews.

A story collected by folklorist George Paterson seems to record the inauguration of Creggan as a burial place in the Middle Ages. The story goes that certain mourners were about to bury a dead friend in Killyloughran (an ancient circular burial ground) when they heard a bell tolling in the distance. They took it as a warning to stop the burial, lifted the remains and, guided by the tolls of the bell, followed it to the spot where Creggan parish church now stands. They buried the remains there. They said the bell was taken as a token of God's command to build a church there and it remains there still.

Sources: Donaldson J., 1923, 83; Paterson T.G.F., 1945, 64; Carville G., *Creggan: a Celtic Christian Site,* Dundalk, 1996; Manning C., *JCLAS* 23, 1996, 512.

㉖ GOWARD DOLMEN

MONUMENT TYPE	Portal Tomb
LOCATION	Near Hilltown, just off Castlewellan Road
GRID REFERENCE	J2437 3104
MONUMENT NUMBER	48:11
STATUS	State Care DOENI (EHS)

Goward Dolmen is an unusual Neolithic stone tomb, attractively sited in a now tree-lined enclosure, on a low north-facing slope, in the foothills of the Mourne Mountains. Built around five thousand years ago by Neolithic farming communities, it is regarded as a very important monument in the region, displaying elements associated with both court tombs and portal tombs. Goward – *Guthard* – means

The Night Sower of Goward

the resounding height, and the name may be derived from a strong echo reputed to be heard in the vicinity of the dolmen.

The dolmen's massive capstone, now slipped from its original position, would have roofed the long rectangular chamber. The chamber walls are 0.9m high and a blocking or end stone stands 1.5m high. The capstone is huge, measuring 1.6m thick; its upper end rests on two tall portal stones, which form the 'doorway' to the chamber. It has been suggested that the portal stones, together with others in and near the field wall, may be the remains of a curving façade of upright stones. This feature is typical of court tombs, which have a number of upright stones defining the court area, and at Goward this may illustrate links between the two monument types – court tombs and portal tombs. This site has not been excavated, although investigations before 1834 uncovered a cremation urn and a flint arrowhead. Traces of the cairn, which would originally have covered the stone chamber, can still be seen around the dolmen, standing in places over 1m high.

The 'Night Sower of Goward' was a ghostly figure who used to be seen sowing seed from a white sheet in the pale moonlight. It is said to be the ghost of a farm labourer who had been murdered and buried hereabouts. This crime was uncovered only when the farmer who owned

The collapsed capstone, Goward Dolmen

the land was ploughing the ground where the murdered man's body lay. The remains were brought to the cemetery close by and laid to rest, and from that time on the 'Night Sower of Goward' was seen no more.

Locally the dolmen is known as 'Pat Kearney's Big Stone' or 'Finn's Finger Stone'. Pat Kearney formerly owned the land and the last traces of his stone house can still be seen beside the dolmen. Finn McCool is reputed to have thrown the stone from Spelga Dam, almost 4km away. It is also reported that Finn is buried under the stone.

Sources: *ASCD* 1966, 79-80; Crowe W.H., *The Ring of Mourne,* Dundalk, 1969, 104-6.

㉗ KILFEAGHAN DOLMEN

MONUMENT TYPE	Portal Tomb
LOCATION	Kilfeaghan, near Rostrevor
GRID REFERENCE	J2322 1535
MONUMENT NUMBER	55:18
STATUS	State Care DOENI (EHS)

The massive capstone of Kilfeaghan Dolmen – note the two portal stones left of centre

This impressive dolmen is sited on a south-facing slope in the lower foothills of the Mourne Mountains overlooking Carlingford Lough. Views over the Mourne coastal plain and the Cooley Mountains can be enjoyed from this monument. It stands on the border of the ancient Kingdom of Mourne and lies in the hinterland below Knockshee, the Fairy Hill, and within a stone's throw of the border river, the Cassy Water.

The massive capstone, estimated to weigh around 35 tons, roofs a chamber formed by three upright and two portal stones. Only the top of the end stone is visible and it has been suggested that the chamber was dug into the slope of the ground and a glacial erratic was used as the roofing stone, propped by the supporting uprights. A small excavation in 1956 revealed that the dolmen was located at the northern end of a stone cairn, which was 33m long and tapered from a width of 10m at the north to 4m at the south. Finds from an unrecorded excavation of the chamber in 1912-14 included bones, flint scrapers and Neolithic pottery.

The name Kilfeaghan is probably derived from the Irish *Cill Fiacháin,* Fiachán's church, but nothing is known about a saint called Fiachán. It has also been suggested that it may mean Féichín's church, and of at least five saints with this name the best known is St Féichín of Fore in Co Westmeath. Both names mean 'little raven'. Local tradition tells that a granite cross, believed to have belonged to a church, was uncovered here many years ago. There is no written or oral tradition of St Fiachán or St Féichín in this area; in fact, local connections are with St Colman, to whom a nearby holy well is dedicated.

Sources: *ASCD* 1966, 80-81; Ó hÓgáin D., *Magic, Myth and Romance,* New York, 1991, 197-198.

28 DONAGHMORE CROSS

MONUMENT TYPE	Cross and Graveyard
LOCATION	Church of Ireland Graveyard, Donaghmore
GRID REFERENCE	J1045 3495
MONUMENT NUMBER	40:37
STATUS	Scheduled Historic Monument

Situated on an eminence overlooking the rolling countryside of south Down is the Church of Ireland parish church of Donaghmore. The church and graveyard are thought to occupy the site of an early ecclesiastical enclosure, and according to William Reeve, who described the site in 1847, the present parish church was built about 18m north of the ancient site. In 1914 the archaeologist J D Cowan reported faint traces of a rath enclosing the graveyard and adjoining paddock and knoll, and remains of a bank can still be seen at the southeast.

Donaghmore Cross, east face

In the graveyard a fine ring-headed granite standing cross stands south of the church. It has been moved at least once during its history and is now among modern headstones and graves. Tradition says it was overthrown in the seventeenth century and the shaft broken into two pieces. It was then re-erected in 1891 and is reputed to stand on the lintel stone of a souterrain or cave, which was closed in 1890. The souterrain apparently ran north-south and was approximately 70m long, with a transept near the centre forming two separate opposing chambers.

On the west face of the cross-head is the crucifixion of Christ, somewhat weathered, but in good light the figures of Christ and the thieves can be seen. On the west face of the shaft are Old Testament scenes, including the figures of Adam and Eve clearly identifiable near the bottom of the shaft. Above Adam and Eve is Noah's ark and above that possibly the sacrifice of Isaac. As the crucifixion often appears with New Testament scenes, it has been suggested that the cross-head may have been reversed when the cross was re-erected; but it has also been suggested that it may belong to another cross.

The east face of the cross-head is carved with a heavily weathered figure, which may be Christ at the Last Judgement, and on the east face of the shaft are figures, including David, and Moses striking water from the rock. On the south face of the shaft is another figure, perhaps David with his harp, and on the north face an unidentified pair of males. The cross can be dated with some confidence to the tenth century.

The name *Domhnach Mór*, the great church, indicates an important early church, probably a centre for very early missionary activity in the area. It was known as *Domhnach Mór Maighe Cobha,* the great church of the plain, which extended far inland to Dromore. It was associated with Mac Erc, a bishop whose festival day is 17 September. Later tradition made him a brother of Mochaoi of Nendrum, a monk who, according to legend, was converted to Christianity by St Patrick, founded an important monastic settlement on the island of Mahee in Strangford Lough, Co Down and died at the end of the fifth century. The see of Armagh held the parish church and lands in medieval times and the rectors and hereditary erenaghs were the McKerrell family. The cross of Donaghmore is a symbol of the prolonged use and worship at this site, and almost fifteen hundred years after the first Christian settlement at *Domhnach Mór* it remains a centre of reverence and prayer for the local community

Sources: Lewis 1837, I, 468; Reeves 1847, 111-12 and 189-90; Cowan J.D., *An Irish Parish, Past and Present, being the Parish of Donaghmore, Co. Down,* London, 1914, 120-28; *ASCD* 1966, 291-2.

29 KILBRONEY CHURCH AND GRAVEYARD

MONUMENT TYPE	Crosses, Church and Graveyard
LOCATION	½km northeast of Rostrevor village
GRID REFERENCE	J1880 1954
MONUMENT NUMBER	51:58
STATUS	Scheduled Historic Monument

Kilbroney Cross – note the intricate fretwork

Kilbroney – *Cill Bhrónaí*, Bronach's church – is a beautiful graveyard sited on a valley side overlooking the Kilbroney River and the pretty seaside village of Rostrevor. St Bronach, the patron saint of the parish, is associated with an early church here. Her feast day is 2 April and she was remembered as 'Bronach, Virgin of *Glenn Sechis*', in Rostrevor.

At the northern edge of the graveyard are the ruins of a church of fifteenth- or sixteenth-century date, with the remains of a nave and chancel. The walls are built of rubble and granite boulders but are greatly obscured by ivy. On the south side of the church among the gravestones are two crosses of differing ages and types.

The larger cross, which stands 2.3 m high, is made of granite and is probably the earliest stone cross in Co Down. It has no ring and its characteristics suggest a wooden model, especially the cut-back 'armpits' and the plain, rounded back. On the front (west) side are panels of fine fretwork, seen clearly only in good diagonal light. Recent research has suggested a date in the late eight or early ninth century.

To the west of the larger earlier cross, among gravestones, is a second, much smaller, cross. It has a wedge-shaped shaft, short stumpy arms and a circular head. Incised on the cross-head are human features including eyes, eyebrows, nose and mouth, and on the arms and shaft is a carved cross. The date of this stone is

An early type of 'face cross'?

disputed: some believe it to be a very early type of 'face cross', while others believe it is a post-medieval gravestone.

Located on lower ground, southwest of the church, is a holy well dedicated to St Bronach. A shrine or grotto of modern date has been erected over the well. The traditional explanation of the holy well is that when St Bronach was killed here by pirates, the present spring burst out of the ground on the spot where she fell. It is said that every year on the anniversary of her death the waters would surge up, overflowing into the meadow below. Many healing virtues and wonderful powers are ascribed to the well. One of these is that it can make someone young and beautiful, and in order to achieve this the person must bathe his or her face in the well at midnight on the eve of Bronach's festival.

The best-known and most dramatic story about the area concerns St Bronach's Bell. The bell, an ancient Celtic bell made of bronze, was originally installed in the forked branches of a tree and was rung to call the faithful to prayer. During a Viking raid on the area the monastery was destroyed and the bell was forgotten. Other trees and bushes soon surrounded the tree and, although the bell could be heard ringing in the wind, no one could find it. It became known as 'the ghost bell'. If the bell rang in the morning it was for joy and if it was heard at funerals it was a sign that the departed rested in peace. One day the bell was heard no more, and as new generations were told the stories about the bell, they dismissed them as 'old wives' tales'. In 1885 an ancient oak tree, which stood near the old church in Kilbroney cemetery, was blown down. When workmen went to saw it up they found a bell embedded in the trunk. The reason for the silencing of the bell was then explained: the ring holding the tongue of the bell had worn away and had fallen down to the bottom of the tree. The very fine cast-bronze bell can now be seen in the sanctuary of St Bronagh's Roman Catholic church in Rostrevor village.

Sources: *ASCD* 1966, 303, pls 73 and 83; Crawford S., *Mourne Rambles, A Cusle na nGael* Supplement, 1994, 6-7.

30 GREENCASTLE

MONUMENT TYPE	Castle
LOCATION	Greencastle, south-west of Kilkeel
GRID REFERENCE	J2473 1184
MONUMENT NUMBER	57:03
STATUS	State Care DOENI (EHS)

Greencastle – *Caisleán na hOireanaí*, the castle of the cultivated place – is a strategically located Norman castle on the summit of a rocky outcrop at the northern entrance of Carlingford Lough. The elevated site of the castle provides extensive views over the lough, the Mourne coastal plain and the majestic Mountains of Mourne to the north. It has been described as 'the best example of fully developed thirteenth-century military architecture in the County'.

The castle occupies an area of about 4 hectares and was originally enclosed by a ditch cut into the rock. Access to the castle was from the south, and at this point the ditch has been partly revealed by excavation, measuring an impressive 3.5m deep, 7m wide at the top

Greencastle

and narrowing to 3m wide at the base. The curtain wall is now largely ruined, and originally it had four towers, one at each corner, but only the plan of the northeast tower is fully visible.

The keep or hall is a large rectangular building measuring 18m by 8.5m internally, with walls nearly 2m thick, originally approached at first-floor level through a forebuilding. Although thirteenth-century in origin, the keep has been altered at various dates, most substantially in the fifteenth and sixteenth centuries. Three cross walls of fifteenth-century date divide the ground floor into three vaults. The first floor or Great Hall originally had small windows, a fireplace and a latrine in the northeast angle. The windows were altered and enlarged in the fifteenth and sixteenth centuries, and in the fifteenth century the upper parts of the keep were heightened and corner turrets were added. A spiral staircase in the southwest angle leads to the wall-walk, to chambers in the turrets and to latrines.

Reconstruction drawing of Greencastle

Built by the Norman, Hugh de Lacy in the middle of the thirteenth century to defend the southern approach to his Earldom, this 'royal castle' has had an eventful history. It was apparently destroyed in 1260 and subsequently repaired. Later the castle was held by the de Burghs, Earls of Ulster; it was captured in 1316 by Edward Bruce, recovered for the king, and attacked at least twice by the Irish in the fourteenth century. In 1505 the castle was granted to the Earl of Kildare and in 1552 was included in a grant of land to Nicholas Bagenal. Although having a tower-house in Newry, Bagenal used Greencastle as his main residence. He is responsible for inserting the large windows in the first floor of the keep and adjoining domestic buildings, of which only fragments survive.

There is a story told about the 'ghost of the castle'. One wild winter's morning a strange boat pulled alongside Greencastle pier and a man dressed in summer clothing came ashore and made his way to the old castle. He never came out again. That night, precisely at twelve o'clock and for a long time after that at the same time every night, the castle cattle kept roaring and trying to escape from their pens. The pots and pans in the castle house rattled and once an old eight-day clock fell off the wall and never worked again. A council of clergy eventually got together and agreed to perform an exorcism. The ghost was banished for five hundred and twenty years. Many local people say the ghost pleaded that he should be banished for only twenty years but the clergy stuck to their guns. The ghost, who is believed to be the mystery visitor, is due back to the castle one of these days!

There is also a famous poem, 'The maid of Mourne Shore', composed by an admirer of Mary Mc Ceon from Greencastle. Mary was the daughter of the miller of Mill Bay and he also had the tavern named 'The Wheat Sheaf Inn'. Mary's mother died at childbirth, and a wandering astrologer left a parchment sealed in a bag with the instructions that it was not to be opened until the child was twenty-one years old. Mary was loved by all and pursued by most of the young men. A fisherman, Joseph Mac Cunigem, won her hand, but on the day of the wedding her father became very ill and they had to cancel the arrangements. The date was rearranged and they decided to marry on Mary's twenty-first birthday. Some days before the wedding, a hurricane arose and it was feared that all the fishermen, including Joseph Mac Cunigem, were lost. On the eve of her wedding Mary went to the shore, hoping that her husband-to-be would return safely with the tide, but instead his body was washed ashore. Overcome with grief, Mary was caught by the tide and swept away. Local people found the bodies of the two lovers the next morning. It is said that the sight of the two bodies killed her father also. Remembering the astrologer's parchment, relatives located the bag and opened it. The parchment read: 'This girl will die before she is twenty-one years old'.

Sources: Waterman D.M. and Collins A.E.P., *UJA* 15, 1952, 87-102; Fitzpatrick W.J., *Mourne Observer*, 1963, 5-8; *ASCD* 1966, 211-19; Crowe W.H., *The Ring of Mourne*, Dundalk, 1969, 75-7; Gaskell-Brown C., *UJA* 42, 1979, 51-65.

③① THE CROWN MOUND

MONUMENT TYPE	Motte and Bailey
LOCATION	Sheeptown, near (northeast of) Newry
GRID REFERENCE	J1074 2791
MONUMENT NUMBER	47:47
STATUS	Scheduled Historic Monument

Infra-red photo of The Crown Mound –
the motte and bailey is the clump of trees
(white) on the top of the hill

The Crown Mound is prominently located on the summit of a north-south ridge overlooking the Clanrye River to the west. Flat meadowland surrounds it on all sides. The Owenmoy River runs through the meadowland and opens out in two branching arms to encircle the 'inch' in the centre of which rises the Mound. The early name for the Mound seems to have been *Ráth Cruithne*, the rath of the Picts, but in its present form the monument can be described as an Anglo-Norman earthwork castle, although archaeologist Tom McNeill has suggested that the Crown Mound may have been built as a fortified centre for the Magennis kings of Iveagh.

This site is very overgrown and difficult to see. It consists of a motte, which is a large pudding- shaped earth mound, surrounded by a waterlogged ditch, and a square bailey to the south. The oval motte summit measures 20m by 13m and stands 15m above the ditch. Although now entirely made of earth, this was probably once topped with wooden structures and surrounded by wooden palisade fencing.

Three stone-lined burial galleries at Annaghmare Court Tomb, Co Armagh

Clontygora Court Tomb - 'The King's Ring'

Ballykeel Dolmen, near Mullaghbane

The Village Cross, Tynan, Co Armagh

Kilnasaggart Pillar Stone, south of
Jonesborough village

Lisleitrim Fort (r) and the crannog in Lisleitrim Lough (l). The proximity of
the two has led archaeologists to suggest that this was a royal site

St Mochua's Well, Derrynoose is a site for local pilgrimage

The ivy-covered remains of Ballymoyer Old Church

Creggan Churchyard – the Eastwood family vault, left of centre,
may be an Early Christian Church

The burial gallery of Goward Dolmen, Co Down

Above: Possibly an early
type of 'face cross' in
Kilbroney graveyard

Right: Donaghmore
Cross, west face

The restored St Mochta's House with St Mary's Priory in the background

Castletown Motte - Dún Dealgan, showing the folly built in 1780 by the pirate, Patrick Byrne

An example of rock art at Drumirril, Co Monaghan

King John's Castle, Carlingford Village, Co Louth

The bailey is 50m long and tapers in width from 42m to 40m. This area was also enclosed by a wooden palisade and probably housed soldiers, horses and supplies.

Local folklore claims that the mound was an arena on which two royal brothers fought for the possession of the crown of *Glenn Righe*. The twin sons of Fearon Garb (Fearon the Fierce) both laid claim to be chief of *Glenn Righe* when their father was killed in battle. Arcu and Aedh each claimed the other was an impostor. The brothers set up armies and faced each other in the valley of the Owenmoy. On the morning of the battle Arcu, realising that the war would destroy their people, challenged his brother to single combat. As both armies wished to see and enjoy the momentous encounter, they agreed to erect a platform for the combatants to settle their dispute. The brothers fought for ten days. Aedh gave Arcu a severe wound in the side but just as it seemed that Arcu would die, he thrust his blade through Aedh's heart, killing him instantly. Arcu, finding that he had killed his brother, exclaimed 'What is victory or life or crown to me, where is my brother dearer than them all?' and, taking his dagger, he plunged it into his own breast and fell beside the lifeless body of Aedh. The two brothers were buried on the mount of the Crown.

> Make their Mount in form a crown
> Rising o'er the fields of Down;
> Lay their swords and dirks so bright,
> By them ready for the fight.
> Beneath them set, where neither frown
> Cause of all the strife and woe;
> That brought the sons of Fearon low
> Glenn Rig's shield no more you are
> Riding in your battle car,
> In your wake the fallen dead,
> To Glenree's foes a cause of dread.
> Never more in wards red tide,
> Shall you battle side by side;

Heroes in the fiercest fray,
Chiefs that ever won the day.
For all the time last your renown,
While stands the Mote of the Crown.
(Irish Folklore Collection, from M.G.Crawford's *Legendary
Stories of the Carlingford Lough District*, Newry, 1996, 108)

Sources: *ASCD* 1966, 206; Crawford M.G., 1996, 104-9.

㉜ NARROW WATER CASTLE

MONUMENT TYPE	Tower-House and Bawn
LOCATION	Narrow Water, near Warrenpoint
GRID REFERENCE	J1265 1935
MONUMENT NUMBER	51:44
STATUS	State Care DOENI (EHS)

Narrow Water Castle – *Caisleán
an Chaoil*, the castle of the narrow
(water) – is strategically located
near Warrenpoint on the north
bank of the Newry River. The
castle is a sixteenth-century
tower-house and bawn, built on a
rocky outcrop, known locally as
Duncarrig, the fort of the rock.
Hemmed in by the imposing
Mountains of Mourne and the
Cooley Mountains, the castle
guards the narrows where the
river enters Carlingford Lough.

The castle from 'Harper's Ferry'

Lassara and the minstrel

The castle is built of split-stone rubble with granite and limestone dressings. It stands three stories high with an attic and measures internally 11.2m by 10.1m. The entrance, located at the west, is defended by a machicolation and leads to a lobby, which has a 'murder hole' above it in the corbelled vault. A stair in the wall thickness leads to the first floor chamber, which is stone-vaulted and has a latrine in the west corner. Above this is another chamber and the wall-walk. The castle remained in use until the eighteenth century and the windows have been much altered. The enclosing bawn, built of stone rubble, is contemporary with the tower-house but was also altered. It is an irregular rectangle in shape and encloses an area of about 36m square. The walls of the bawn are over half a metre thick and stand 2m high above the interior.

Written sources record that in 1568 John Sancky was warder of the castle and had a garrison of four kern (lightly armed foot-soldiers). In the following year he had twelve kern, and from the summer of 1569 to the spring of 1570 he also had six horsemen.

Sancky was paid £36 4s 2d for building and fortifying the castle and in 1570 was granted a lease of the castle for a period of twenty-one years. His stewardship does not appear to have lasted long, however, as in 1580 Hugh Magennis was in residence. By 1608 the castle had again changed hands and was held by Sir Arthur Magennis.

A local legend tells of Lassara, the daughter of Conn MacGuinness, supreme commander of the Clan MacGuinness. She fell in love with a wandering minstrel and decided to elope with him to his keep in Loch Ochter (Scotland). They boarded a skiff (a small boat) and, as they drifted past the tower-house at Narrow Water, a sentry spotted them. He fired at the couple and an arrow struck the minstrel, who fell over the low side of the skiff, clasping his harp to his breast. Lassara was captured and put in the dungeon of the castle. At night, alone in the prison, she believed she could hear the harp strains from her musician lover, sounding wildly in the dash of the waves, as if he were serenading her. The warden of the tower-house was making unwelcome advances towards her and threatened to put her to death unless she married him. He gave her one week to agree to his proposal. On the last night of the week, as the warden opened the dungeon door, Lassara darted past him and made her way up to the top of the castle. She leapt from the top of the tower and, as she dropped to the icy water below, it is said that the music of the harper could be heard, drawing Lassara to him. She perished in the place where her minstrel lover had died.

The news reached the MacGuinness camp and Conn rallied his clansmen. They attacked the castle and managed to drive the surviving garrison members up to the top of the tower. The warden, seeing that all was lost, took his life by jumping from the tower into the water and drowning where Lassara and the harper had died. It is said that often at night the music of the harper mingles with the sound of the waves, and that at the place known as 'Harper's Ferry' Lassara and her lover can be seen.

Sources: *ASCD* 1966, 241-3; Crawford S., *Mourne Rambles, A Cusle na nGael* Supplement, 1994, 22; Crawford M.G., 1996, 31-4.

33 PROLEEK DOLMEN

MONUMENT TYPE	Portal Tomb
LOCATION	In the grounds of the Ballymascanlan Hotel
GRID REFERENCE	J083 111
MONUMENT NUMBER	LH004:074
STATUS	National Monument

Proleek – *an thaobh leac*, the stone of the hillside – is a small townland north of Dundalk, overlooking the Flurry River. The impressive tomb known as Proleek Dolmen can be found set on a river terrace to the west of the river, at the north edge of Ballymascanlan golf-course. Ballymascanlan (McScanlan's townland) takes its name from Scanlan, son of Fingin, chief of the Uí Meith sept. This sept had extensive holdings in Co Louth and gave its name to the village of Omeath.

The dolmen at Proleek has a capstone weighing approx 40 tons

This is an impressive dolmen, with a massive capstone measuring 3.8m by 3.2m and estimated to weigh about 40 tons. It rests on two portal stones standing 2.3m high, and a side stone which has been strengthened using a stone and concrete support. The chamber faces northwest and there are no visible remains of a cairn. Nearby in the same field is a good example of a wedge tomb.

Local tradition holds that if you successfully land one stone in three on top of the capstone you will be married before the year is out, and there are always stones thrown on its top! Popular tradition also claims that the giant, Parra Buí MacShane, lies here after his fatal encounter with the famous Finn McCool.

Sources: Borlase 1897, 305-7; *Tempest*, 1952, 72-3; *ASCL* 1991, 34-5.

③④ CLERMONT CAIRN

MONUMENT TYPE	Passage Tomb
LOCATION	On the summit of Black Mountain, west of Omeath village
GRID REFERENCE	J098 157
MONUMENT NUMBER	LH004:004
STATUS	National Monument

Clermont Cairn — *Carn na breid naire*, the heap of shamed stones — is located high in the hills above Ravensdale on the southwest summit of Black Mountain (510m). A now ruinous passage tomb over 4,500 years old, this cairn was once a significant local landmark. When you have reached the cairn there are extensive views over Carlingford Lough to the east and the Ring of Gullion to the northwest.

The cairn is built of boulders

Clermont Cairn, Ravensdale –
after ASCL, 1991

Northeast aspect of Clermont Cairn

and measures 21m in diameter and over 4m in height. There is no trace of an enclosing kerb, although the surrounding bog may obscure it. A lintelled passage is visible within the cairn, orientated southwest and measuring 3.5m long. On top of the cairn is the ruin of a circular drystone structure that appears to be the remains of a folly built by Lord Clermont, a local landlord who resided at Ravensdale House, now demolished.

There are many other sites of interest in the vicinity of Clermont Cairn. Lissachiggel (the fort of the rye) is an old circular stone-built village enclosure containing foundations of stone huts; the Cadgers' Road is a path along which the herring sellers from Omeath travelled nearly a hundred years ago, their donkeys loaded with creels of fish. Carnavaddy Mountain rises above this path and on its summit is another cairn (the Hound's Cairn), and it is here that Bran, Finn McCool's loyal dog, is said to be buried.

Southeast of Clermont is a popular picnic area in the Cooley Mountains, known as 'The Long Woman's Grave', probably the site of a destroyed court tomb. The tomb is associated with a local legend about Lorcan O'Hanlon, one of the O'Hanlon sept of south Armagh. He went to Spain and married a lady of high position. He boasted to her of his vast estates back home in Ireland and when they arrived at the 'Windy Gap' the lady, who it is said was very tall, dropped dead with shock at the sight of the barren bogs and mountains. Lorcan, consumed with grief, threw himself into the nearby marsh. The spot where the young woman fell has been recorded in local history as 'the Long Woman's Grave'.

Sources: *CLAJ* 1941, 77-9; *CLAJ* 1981, 49; Herity M., 1977, 232; *ASCL* 1991, 37-8; Murphy M.J., 1975, 102.

35 St Mochta's House

MONUMENT TYPE	Early Church
LOCATION	Northern edge of Louth village
GRID REFERENCE	H955 014
MONUMENT NUMBER	LH115:002
STATUS	National Monument

An early church, known as St Mochta's House, survives in a field behind the extensive ruins of the Augustinian Abbey on the northern edge of Louth village. Louth gets its name from the ancient Celtic sun god, *Lugh*, and may have been a place of worship since pagan times.

Mochta, who died in AD536, is claimed as a disciple of St Patrick, but this may merely reflect the close relationship which later developed between Louth and Armagh. Attacks on the church, both by the Irish and the Vikings, are recorded, but the community seems to have flourished. Louth village was burned in 1111, 1133 and 1148, and the stone church dates from later in the twelfth century. In 1148 Louth was refounded as a priory of Augustinian Canons and substantial remains of their buildings can be seen across the field.

St Mochta's House with St Mary's Priory in the background

St Mochta's House is a small rectangular church measuring internally 4.88m by 2.82m. A barrel vault of small thin slabs covers the church and above this is a croft or chamber with a pointed roof. Access to the croft is by a short and very narrow stone stairway in the northwest corner of the church. It is likely that this stone church replaced an earlier, probably wooden, structure which contained St Mochta's remains. Churches with the name 'house', like this one and St Molaise's House on Devenish (Co Fermanagh), are thought to be closely associated with the founder's relics.

St Mochta's House was extensively restored in 1934 and the enclosing wall was built in 1906. Large gaps in the east and west walls of the church were closed with masonry and a door at ground level and window in the croft were inserted. This restoration can be seen clearly as the new stonework is recessed behind the original work.

St Daig, associated with Inishkeen in Co Monaghan (46), is said to have visited St Mochta in Louth. Mochta predicted that 'many a church vessel in gold, in silver, in brass and in iron shall proceed from this youth's hand. Many an eloquent volume shall it write. That hand shall also administer the Body and Blood of Christ to me in the Holy Communion when I am about to be called out of this world', and tradition tells that St Daig was present at the death of St Mochta.

Sources: *CLAJ* 1937, 32-5; Leask H.G., *Irish Churches and Monastic Buildings* I, Dundalk, 1955, 40; *ASCL* 1991, 252-4; Duffy P.J., 1993, 98-9.

36 LOUTH ABBEY

MONUMENT TYPE	Augustinian Abbey
LOCATION	The edge of Louth village
GRID REFERENCE	J957 014
MONUMENT NUMBER	LH115:005
STATUS	National Monument No.970

The first church at Louth was founded by St Mochta in the sixth century, traditionally on the site of a Druid's Grove. Monastic settlement was revived at Louth in 1148, under the patronage of Donnchad O'Carroll, King of Oriel, in association with Edan O'Kelly, Bishop of Louth. They established Augustinian Canons in St Mary's Priory. Much is known from written sources about this community and a detailed description of its buildings and lands survives from the time it

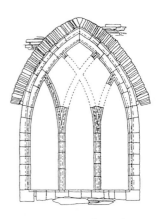

South window of chancel,
St Mary's Priory, Louth – after ASCL,
1991

The fourteenth-century church at St Mary's Priory

surrendered to King Henry VIII in 1539 and was dissolved. To the south of the site is a wooded Anglo-Norman motte, constructed before 1196, and reputed to have been visited by King John in 1210.

Much of the present medieval church dates from the fourteenth century. It is very long and narrow, over 46m long, and was originally divided by a cross-wall into a nave, for the parish, and a chancel, for the canons. A remnant of this wall projects from the south wall. The gable walls and south wall survive, but much of the north wall has gone and is replaced by a modern stone wall.

Of special interest are the ornate church windows of moulded and diagonally-tooled limestone. The window in the east gable has been partly filled, but apparently had four lights (openings) and complex tracery. It was inserted into the blocking of a once much larger window, the arch of which can be clearly seen reaching nearly to the top of the gable. There are five windows in the south wall; two of the four in the former chancel have three lights and plain intersecting tracery. High in the west gable of the former nave was a window (in sandstone) with three lights and plain tracery.

The cloister was on the north side, and joist holes in the surviving remnant of the north wall indicate a building several stories high. A round tower is recorded south of the church, but there are no visible remains of this. Louth Abbey is a remarkable structure surviving in the heart of a pretty, rural village.

Sources: Harbison P., *CLAJ* 18, 1973, 39-42; Bradley J., *CLAJ* 21, 1985, 8-22; *ASCL* 1991, 253-6.

③⑦ Faughart Church and Graveyard

MONUMENT TYPE	Medieval Church, Graveyard and Holy Well
LOCATION	North-west of Dundalk
GRID REFERENCE	J058 127
MONUMENT NUMBER	LH49:702
STATUS	National Monument

Faughart Graveyard is located on a high level terrace on the summit of a drumlin hill, south of Slievenabolea and overlooking Dundalk Bay. The name Faughart has two possible explanations, both relating to the mighty warrior Cú Chulainn and the *Táin Bó Cúailgne*. The first possible source of the name is *Fochard* – 'the place of the great feat', while the second is *Focherd* – 'the good cast' – (see 38 for more details on the name).

The foundation of a convent for nuns in this area is attributed to St Darerca, also known as St Moninna, who is said to have settled here before she went to Killevy (19). Faughart is also reputed to have been the birthplace of Brigid, daughter of the chief Dubtach and a slave girl, Brocessa, around AD453. She is known today as St Brigid, 'Mary of the Gael', whose feast day is on 1 February, taken to be the first day of spring.

In the graveyard are the ruins of a small medieval church with a nave and chancel, St Brigid's Well and two features traditionally known as St Brigid's Pillar and St Brigid's Bed. A preliminary excavation of the site

Infra-red photo of Faughart Graveyard. The church is slightly left of centre, with St Brigid's Pillar in the foreground

in 1966 revealed that the church nave is probably twelfth century, while the chancel is later medieval in date. The nave has some surviving features. The door at the west has been enlarged, but two rough granite blocks are part of the original door surround. There is a window in the north wall and a window jamb high in the south wall above a modern inserted doorway. A 1966 excavation uncovered a trench that ran under the church, perhaps part of a double-ditched enclosure identified by aerial photography.

St Brigid's Pillar was also investigated during this excavation and a circular single course of large stones, 18m in circumference, was uncovered. This has been interpreted as possibly the foundation course of a once substantial round tower. West of the graveyard is St Brigid's Stream, a place of pilgrimage for local people. Here there is a shrine, completed in 1934, and around the stream are stones, which feature in the ritual pilgrimage. People suffering from various diseases come and bathe in the stream and pieces of cloth tied to trees are symbols that some special favours have been prayed for.

Faughart has been the scene of many battles. In one, fought in AD672, Áedh Róin, King of Ulaid was slain, and his head was cut off on the 'Stone of Decapitation' which can be found near the door of the old church. Over six hundred years later another king, Edward Bruce, brother of the famous Robert, lost his Irish throne here and also his head, which was sent to King Edward I. Just two years before his death in 1318, Bruce had crowned himself king of Ireland, allegedly within sight of the place of his death. He is buried in Faughart graveyard.

Sources: Connor L., *CLAJ* 1966, 125-9; Barrow 1979, 154; *ASCLS* 1991, 230-31; Clarke G. and O'Sullivan H., *Dundalk and North Louth*, Cottage Publications, 1997, 24-5.

38 FAUGHART MOTTE

MONUMENT TYPE	Norman Motte
LOCATION	200m northwest of Faughart Graveyard
GRID REFERENCE	J 056 127
MONUMENT NUMBER	LH04:02301
STATUS	Recorded Historic Monument

Faughart Motte stands on top of Faughart Hill, close to Faughart Graveyard and overlooking Dundalk Bay. The first possible meaning of the name Faughart — *Fochard,* the place of the great feat — refers to one of the many battles of Cú Chulainn during the cattle raid of Cooley (Táin Bó Cuailgne). It is said that while Cú Chulainn was encamped in a rath near Dundalk, Queen Maeve secretly hid fourteen of her men at

The motte at Faughart

vantage points around Faughart. She then cunningly lured him out for a parley. When Cú Chulainn finally appeared in the open he was attacked by Maeve's men but he bravely defeated them, hence the 'place of the great feat'. Another source claims that Cú Chulainn fought in single combat against Fer Baeth, one of Maeve's warriors, whom he killed by throwing a holy 'shoot back' over his shoulder, striking Fer Baeth on the nape of the neck, so supporting the explanation *Focherd* – the 'good cast'.

The motte stands 8m high and has a summit diameter of over 15m. It is surrounded by an almost flat-bottomed ditch, 1.5m deep and 6m at its widest extent. The ditch has been encroached on at the northeast by a road. Wright's *Louthiana* of 1758 shows an octagonal enclosure surrounding the summit of the mound and two ramps running out from the mound. Part of the enclosure on the mound has been removed, but a length survives from the northwest to the southeast. This has been interpreted as a possible fortification built by Charles Blount, Lord Deputy Mountjoy, during the Tyrone Rebellion in the early 1600s.

Local tradition tells of an earthwork once belonging to St Brigid's father and his ancestors, where perhaps Cú Chulainn stood, watching and waiting for his opportunity to swoop down on the armies of Maeve. Many years later the Normans came and changed the shape of the mound into the motte and bailey. Excavations of mottes elsewhere have shown that in some cases they were built on the site of earlier earthworks.

Sources: *Tempest* 1952, 101-3; *ASCL* 1991, 286-8.

③⑨ Castletown Motte – Dún Dealgan

MONUMENT TYPE	Motte and Bailey
LOCATION	On Castletown Road, Dundalk
GRID REFERENCE	N0294 0830
MONUMENT NUMBER	LH007:11807
STATUS	National Monument

Could this be the ancient home of Cú Chulainn?

Standing proud on a low hill in Castletown, overlooking the industrial town of Dundalk, is a large well-preserved motte, known locally as *Dún Dealgan*. There is a strong tradition that the great mound of *Dún Dealgan* stands on the site of the house of Cú Chulainn, hero of the Ulster Cycle, although in its present state it is recognised as a Norman motte. The earthworks are believed to have been built in the latter part of the twelfth century by the de Verdun family. The motte is a large, steep-sided mound standing some 10m in height with a summit diameter of 43m. A souterrain is located in the south side of the motte and on top is a folly built in 1780 by the infamous local pirate, Patrick Byrne.

A ditch, measuring at its widest 18.5m, surrounds the motte. The ditch has an external bank, ranging from 3.5m to 5m wide and standing 1.5m high above the local ground level. In a drawing of the site in Wright's *Louthiana* of 1758, two baileys are shown in addition to the motte. The small D-shaped bailey adjoining the ditch at the northwest survives, while the larger, sub-rectangular bailey shown by Wright at the east has been almost totally destroyed by a modern waterworks. There is a 4m-wide gap in the bank at the east side of the mound, with a causeway over the ditch, but it is not clear whether this is an original feature.

In the *Táin Bó Cuailgne* and other stories of the Ulster Cycle, the place called *Delca Muirthemne* can be recognised as the home and last resting place of Cú Chulainn and his wife Emer. In the story 'the Wooing of Emer', we hear how Cú Chulainn won Emer's heart after she had set him a number of tasks. These included him having to perform the feat of the salmon leap and also to deliver a sword stroke which slew several but spared men selectively. Cú Chulainn completed these tasks by attacking Emer's well-guarded home south of the River Boyne in Co Meath. He charged the defenders with a scythe-wheeled chariot and slew 309 of them. He then performed a salmon leap over the rampart and thrice over he slew nine men, sparing one man in the middle of them each time. Although it cannot be proved, this site in Dundalk may well have been Cú Chulainn's home.

Sources: Tempest, 1952, 68-70; *ASCL* 1991, 283.

④ CASTLE ROCHE

MONUMENT TYPE	Castle
LOCATION	7km northwest of Dundalk and 5km southwest of Forkill
GRID REFERENCE	H991 118
MONUMENT NUMBER	LH29:001
STATUS	National Monument

Castle Roche stands guard on the Louth-Armagh border

Spectacularly sited on the western edge of a high inland limestone cliff, Castle Roche stands guard on the Louth-Armagh border, over an ancient route into what is now south Armagh. The castle marks the most northerly extent of the Anglo-Norman Pale and the frontier with the Gaelic province of Ulster.

Lady Rohesia de Verdun is reported to have built a castle in 1236 on her lands. Traditionally this has been identified with Castle Roche, but some sources dispute this date and believe that it was her son, John, who died in 1274, who built it. Archaeologist Tom McNeill supports the earlier date, and points to the close similarity between Beeston Castle in Cheshire and Castle Roche; both are sited on rock outcrops and they have nearly identical gatehouses. He thinks that the design of Castle Roche may have been based on Beeston Castle. Built around 1225, Beeston was unoccupied by 1237 and reverted to the Crown. This supports Lady Rohesia's connection and the 1236 date, as it is unlikely that an unoccupied castle would have been copied. In early records the castle was called *Castellum de Rupe* – the Castle of the Rock. It is said to have been demolished in the seventeenth century by Oliver Cromwell in his campaign to subdue the Irish.

On the east side of the castle a wide, shallow ditch has been cut through the rock, with access by a causeway. A gap in the causeway is now filled in, but it is thought that a drawbridge was located here, possibly protected by a barbican. This provides access through the gatehouse between two protecting semicircular towers. The curtain

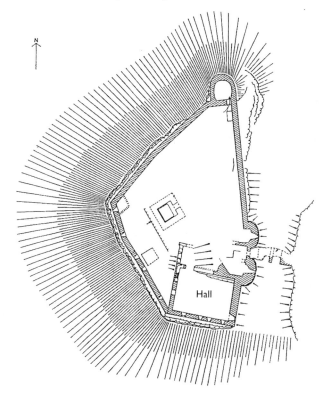

Castle Roche, Co Louth – after ASCL, 1991

wall encloses an area roughly triangular in shape and inside is a hall situated at the south side and the remnants of a freestanding rectangular structure just west of centre. Steep cliffs defend the castle and there is only one tower in the curtain wall, located at the north angle. Much of the curtain wall has well-preserved crenellations, with holes below, either for projecting timbers or for drainage from the wall-walk.

The great hall, now two stories high, may once have had more stories, as the east wall is higher than the other walls, and there is evidence of an additional floor. The three large windows on the first floor all have window-seats. A doorway in the west end of the north wall gave access to the hall and at some stage a small rectangular building or annexe was added to the north side of the hall. Only the western part of this building now survives.

A rectangular structure in the gatehouse is problematic in date and function. It has two surviving levels, a basement or cellar level and a first floor. It has been claimed to be later in date than the rest of the castle structure, but also to be a well-house contemporary with the rest of the castle. Although the semicircular exteriors of the gatehouse towers survive, the interior parts have been destroyed. Each tower originally had four stories with a barrel vault over the ground floor and a gate would have been set between the two towers.

Tradition tells us that when the castle was completed, Rohesia de Verdun had the architect thrown from one of the windows in the north tower to preserve the secrets of the castle's design, and the window is known locally as 'the murder window'. The area around Castle Roche is famous for its rich red earth, which folklore claims was created by the 'Black Pig', said to have traversed Ireland, tearing up a trench as it went ('The Black Pig's Dyke'), thus providing a folkloric explanation of a natural phenomenon. The story goes that the pig was wounded in north Louth and its blood turned the soil red.

Sources: *ASCL* 1991, 333-7; McNeill T., 1997, 85-8 and 166; Clark G. and O'Sullivan H., *Dundalk and North Louth*, Cottage Publications, 1997, 41-2; Tempest, 1952, 110-1.

41 KING JOHN'S CASTLE

MONUMENT TYPE	Castle
LOCATION	Carlingford village
GRID REFERENCE	J188 119
MONUMENT NUMBER	LH005:4202
STATUS	National Monument

King John's Castle in Carlingford harbour

Strategically sited on a high rocky outcrop overlooking Carlingford Lough is the thirteenth-century Norman castle known locally as King John's Castle. Carlingford was called *Cathair Linn*, the Pool City, in early Irish sources. It lies on the southwest side of the lough facing Greencastle (30) to the east, and local tradition claims that St Patrick landed here on his second visit to Ireland. Tradition also claims that he travelled from Carlingford when he went to preach the Christian message on the Isle of Man.

The castle is roughly oval in plan and its earliest part dates from about AD1200. Its curtain wall on the west encloses a D-shaped courtyard some 30m across. A gatehouse with two rectangular towers protected the entrance on the west side, but only part of the northern tower now survives. A rectangular tower is located at the southwest

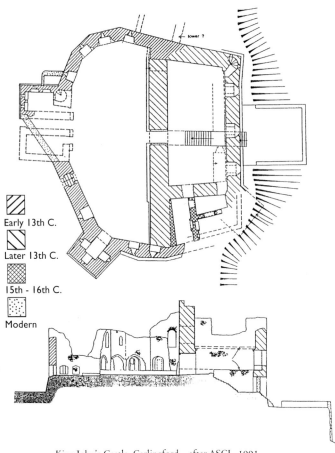

King John's Castle, Carlingford – after ASCL, 1991

corner of the curtain wall and there may have been three other projecting towers: on the north, at the southeast corner and to the east above the cliff. The curtain wall is pierced by a series of narrow openings set in rectangular embrasures. These also occur in the gatehouse, in the southwest tower, and at the first-floor level. The earliest buildings in this enclosure must have been made of wood.

A massive, 3m-wide cross-wall divides the site from north to south and the eastern area of the castle was redeveloped. One theory is that this was done in about 1262, when expenditure on the castle is recorded, but it has also been suggested that it was a fifteenth-century reworking of the castle. There is also disagreement about the use of the rooms east of the cross-wall. Some claim that the building provided a hall and chamber for the thirteenth-century castle, but another view is that by the fifteenth century the castle had retreated to the area behind (east of) the cross-wall, which has crenellations, and that this was a late medieval range (of two stories above a basement). Later the castle was involved in seventeenth-century warfare and was used by Frederick Herman, Duke of Schomberg, as a hospital.

Although traditionally associated with King John, who stayed here for three days in 1210, the castle was almost certainly begun by Hugh de Lacy, some years before John's arrival.

A local story about de Lacy and his daughter is linked to King John's Castle. It is said that de Lacy's daughter was promised to de Burgo, another Norman noble whom he wanted to succeed him as Earl of Ulster. De Lacy's daughter, as so often happens, fell in love with another, known as de Whyte, the Knight of Ballug Castle (Ballug is situated south of Carlingford in Cooley). When de Burgo discovered the affair he swore revenge and accused de Whyte of conspiring against Hugh de Lacy. He took him prisoner to Carlingford Castle and proceeded to torture him. De Whyte eventually died, imprisoned in Carlingford Castle. After a period of grief, and ignorant of the role he had played in the death of her lover, the daughter of de Lacy married de Burgo. It was soon whispered amongst the garrison in the castle of Carlingford that the footsteps of the murdered Knight of Ballug could be heard coming from the torture chamber, walking along the corridors and up and down the turret steps.

Lady de Burgo eventually found out about the circumstances of de Whyte's death and she left her husband. The lonely man, waiting in vain to hear his wife's returning footsteps, was instead tormented by the footsteps of the man he had tortured and murdered. At last Lady de Burgo forgave her husband and returned, not to Carlingford but to Downpatrick, where they made their new home away from the ghost in the castle. Much later, on Sunday, 6 June 1333 Robert de Mandeville, warden of Carrickfergus Castle, slew William de Burgo, the last Earl of Ulster. William was the last of his line and thus the feud between the de Burgos and the de Whytes was at an end. The 'Whyte Knight' of Ballug was avenged at last and the footsteps on the stairs of Carlingford Castle were heard no more.

Sources: Crawford M.G., 1996, 27-30 ; *ASCL* 1991, 320-23; McNeill T., 1997, 40-44 and 192-3; Tempest, 1952, 81-7; Harbison P., 1992, 159-60.

42 DUNMAHON CASTLE

MONUMENT TYPE	Tower-house
LOCATION	South of Dundalk near the railway line. Note that the castle is dangerous and should only be viewed from outside
GRID REFERENCE	J0361 0205
MONUMENT NUMBER	LH012:018
STATUS	Recorded Historic Monument

Dunmahon Castle is a medieval tower-house located on a level terrace overlooking a small tributary of the River Fane. It is four stories high, built of greywacke and limestone rubble with a wall-walk at roof level, a garderobe tower at the northwest angle and a stair tower at the northeast angle. The tower is entered through a doorway in the north wall, which gives access to the ground floor and the stairs. A murder hole is sited above the entrance for additional defence and the door was secured with a long draw-bar. The ground floor room has a barrel vault, which supports the first floor, but the second and third levels had wooden floors.

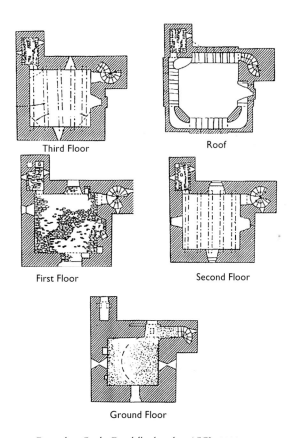

Third Floor

Roof

First Floor

Second Floor

Ground Floor

Dunmahon Castle, Dundalk - based on ASCL, 1991

An incident connected with the castle has helped to preserve its name in local folklore. It concerns the daughter of Fitz-Walters, a local Anglo-Norman chief who owned the castle around 1641. Fitz-Walters resisted all challenges from Oliver Cromwell, who had reduced Drogheda to ruins, and, while Cromwell wanted to take the castle, he had no wish to harm it. He engineered that one of his officers, Captain Charles Townley, should form a liaison with Fitz-Walters' daughter, Eva, and she soon fell in love with him. One night she gave him the keys of the castle as a sign of her love and devotion. Townley used the keys to help his army gain access to the castle where they slaughtered all the inhabitants – all, that is, except Eva. She pleaded with Townley not to abandon her, but he told her: 'she, who sold her father and mother, the priest and his flock for the love of him, would most likely act in a similar way towards himself, if her foolish passion were equally tampered with by another'. A local poem recalls the event:

> Three hundred and nine without falsehood assembled in it
> Of people who loved not wile or deceit
> They were all lost, the good priest along with them
> Through the deceit and false pride of the wicked woman that is
> now wretched.

Sources: Tempest 1952, 114; *ASCL* 1991, 311-13.

43 MULLYASH CAIRN

MONUMENT TYPE	Cairn – possible Passage Tomb
LOCATION	Summit of Mullyash Mountain, in a modern forestry plantation
GRID REFERENCE	H8693 2583
MONUMENT NUMBER	MN15:07
STATUS	National Monument No.564

Mullyash Cairn is located on the summit of a hilltop, among the trees of a modern forestry plantation. In the past it commanded extensive views over Monaghan, Armagh and Tyrone, and the monument builders' reasons for siting it here over 4,000 years ago are obvious. Today all the views are obstructed by the modern forest, which is unfortunately encroaching on the monument itself, and the cairn's landscape setting has been completely lost.

The cairn is composed of small- to medium-sized boulders, and measures 16m in diameter and 1.85m high. The perimeter is neatly

Mullyash Cairn is believed to cover a Neolithic passage tomb

revetted in a technique reminiscent of drystone-walling, where the stones are laid upon each other in a method which requires no mortar. Stones have tumbled in places beyond the kerb line, but in general this is a remarkably well-preserved site. There is a depression in the cairn which appears to follow a path from north-northwest to south-southeast, and this may indicate a passageway. West of centre is a more clearly defined circular hollow, some 0.7m deep, which could mark the position of a tomb.

In 1879, the historian and antiquarian Evelyn Phillip Shirley reported that a cairn in Knocknaneen (the adjoining townland), which had been opened in 1816, was found to contain human bones and a pottery vessel. There is no known cairn in the townland of Knocknaneen and it is possible that this account may refer to the Mullyash cairn. It has been suggested that this is a passage tomb, similar to those at Clermont (34), or Knockmany in the Clogher valley, Co Tyrone.

Mullyash Cairn is traditionally said to contain the remains of a princess whose father would not allow her to marry a prince who loved her. The two eloped and were followed by the king and his army. The princess was killed during the chase and they buried her body at

Mullyash. Some believed that treasure was buried with her and so when people went to see where the princess was buried each took a stone to put on her grave, possibly to protect it from grave-robbers, and that is why there is a cairn at Mullyash.

The nearby townland of Lurganearly is said to have got its name from a stone on Mullyash Mountain. The stone bore the footprint of an earl, hence the name *Lorg an Iarla*, the footprint of the earl. The last Sunday in July and the first Sunday in August are traditionally associated with the festival of Lughnasa and are known locally as 'Blaeberry Sundays'. On these Sundays throngs of people would climb to the top of the mountain gathering blaeberries (blueberries). The expedition would stop at the cairn and it was always a festive occasion, with singing, dancing and sports.

Sources: Livingstone P., 1980, 11, 13, 152, 495; Glassie H., *Passing the Time, Folklore and History of an Ulster Community*, Dublin, 1982, *AICM* 1984, 96; Duffy P.J., 1993; MacNeill M., *The Festival of Lughnasa*, Dublin, 1982, I, 161-3.

44 DRUMIRRIL ROCK ART

MONUMENT TYPE	Rock Art
LOCATION	South of Inishkeen – see Patrick Kavanagh Centre for directions and advice about visits
GRID REFERENCE	H93 04
MONUMENT NUMBER	MN32:19
STATUS	Recorded Historic Monument

In a rocky area known as the 'Deerpark', a minimum of seventy examples of rock art can be seen on at least five rock outcrops. The designs range from a seven-ringed cup and ring with a radial groove to simple cup-shaped hollows. It was not necessarily the prominent rock outcrops that were most heavily decorated; indeed some relatively inconspicuous outcrops are intensively marked on every angle with

Rock with seven-ringed cup motif

single cups in linear arrangements.

These *petroglyphs* or *rock-scribings* (rock art) — generally assigned to the Bronze Age — may share at least some functions and origins wih the art of the Neolithic passage tombs. However, while their distribution around the coastline and at different altitudes is similar to the distribution pattern of passage tombs, their function is more mysterious. Often these petroglyphs relate to natural solution-pits in rocks and boulders, which were frequently enhanced by rings, hence the term cup and ring. They are obviously not 'cultic' like the relatively easy-to-interpret stones of the Iron Age, but their significance remains largely enigmatic.

The most commonly found motif is the cup-and-ring or cup and partial ring, and surfaces with this motif tend to be near places where copper or gold ores were mined. With the recent rediscovery of gold-bearing strata nearby at Clontibrit, Co Monaghan, is it possible that these early metal workers exploited these resources over 3,000 years ago? One thing remains certain: these sites had a mystic and ritual significance which fitted in with funeral rites, early astronomy and metal-mining.

Unfortunately, some of the surrounding land where rock art was recorded in the past has been subjected to reclamation, and much of the rock has been cleared away. It is also likely that the building of the Deerpark wall would have involved local stone quarrying and the possible destruction of even more decorated stones.

Petroglyphic rocks and stones are one of the most unusual and enigmatic of the archeological monuments in this book. This is because their locations are no longer significant, our understanding of their importance is very limited, and their nature presents endless possible interpretations of their function — as maps, astrological charts and signposts — even if, like the rock art on this site, it has been forgotten and now lies in the middle of an inconspicuous field.

Sources: *CLAJ* 1982, 16-17; *AICM* 1986, 10; *CLAJ* 1985, 73-109.

45 DONAGH GRAVEYARD

MONUMENT TYPE	Medieval Cross and Church
LOCATION	Southwest of Glaslough village
GRID REFERENCE	H704 409
MONUMENT NUMBER	MN07:07
STATUS	Recorded Historic Monument

Donagh — *Domnach,* meaning Sunday — church is situated in a secluded graveyard on a low hill, in the rolling drumlin landscape southwest of Glaslough village. The early name was *Domnach-maige-dá-chlaoine,* which means the church of the plain of two slopes, but the parish is now known as Donagh. The type of church known as *Domnach* churches were claimed by Armagh to be Patrician foundations, but it is now recognised that most were important early independent churches, which were later drawn into the orbit of Armagh.

This church is documented in the early sixteenth century, when it was clearly the parish church. A violent event took place on St Patrick's Day in 1508, when the church was attacked during a service, fires were started, and the attackers were killed. By 1662 the church was reported to be standing 'inconveniently ruinous [in] a bog and a wood far from ye Plantation', and a new church was built in Glaslough village, where the Church of Ireland parish church now stands.

In the graveyard are the ruined, overgrown and largely featureless remains of the church, with a cross-wall cutting it in two. Near the graveyard gate is a stone cross, discovered by local landlord, Shane Leslie, and set up on a new concrete base in 1911. It is an unperforated ringed cross with a rather irregular

Unperforated ringed cross with crucified figure

outline on a fairly short, perhaps incomplete, shaft. On the main face of the cross-head is a crucified figure, primitive in style, with the head and body full-face and the legs and feet in profile. The ring is decorated with chevrons. On the back there is no decoration and only the outline of the cross is delineated. This cross is not included in most discussions of early, so-called 'high' crosses, and it is likely to date from the Middle Ages, perhaps as late as the sixteenth century. True 'high crosses' are usually dated to the early Christian period; ninth–twelfth centuries. These normally have sculptural inscriptions and were associated with early churches and monastic sites.

Also in Donagh graveyard is an early cross-base, its socket often filled with water, and part of an early cross-head is also reported. A particular feature are the fine headstones, often carved with crests of families like the McKennas and the McMahons. Pilgrimages to St Patrick's Well at Donagh were popular and there are many stories of cures and favours from this well and another St Patrick's Well at Annahean nearby. A bronze processional cross, found in a nearby bog, is now on display at Monaghan County Museum.

Sources: Davies O., *UJA 2, 1939*, 26-8; *AICM* 1986, 85; Duffy P.J., 1993, 70-1.

46 INISHKEEN ROUND TOWER

MONUMENT TYPE	Round Tower
LOCATION	Church of Ireland graveyard, Inishkeen
GRID REFERENCE	H933 070
MONUMENT NUMBER	MN29:31
STATUS	National Monument No.208

Inishkeen is a pretty rural village on the banks of the Fane River. Its early name was *Inis Caoin Dega*, the beautiful island of Daig. Daig mac Carell, who died in AD578, founded a church here and there are references in the annals to burning (in AD789) and plundering (in AD948). A late account of Daig's life claims that he was associated with many prominent churchmen, including Columba of Derry, Molaise of Devenish (Co Fermanagh), Comgall of Bangor (Co Down), Mochta of Louth (35), and Finnian of Clonard. His feast day was 18 August and he was remembered as a craftsman, 'one of the three chief artisans of Ireland', associated with Ciaran of Clonmacnoise:

> one hundred and fifty bells, a triumphant achievement,
> with a stout hostful hundreds of croziers,
> with sixty whole gospels,
> from the hand of Daig alone.

Inishkeen Round Tower at sunset

The ecclesiastical site is on the north edge of the village close to the Fane River, where, according to an account of Daig's life, the monks had a mill. In the graveyard are the remains of a round tower, much altered and lacking any distinguishing features, but perhaps dating from the tenth or eleventh century. Built of roughly-coursed limestone blocks, it is about 12.6m high, 4.5m in diameter at the base and the door sill is about 4m above the ground. No windows survive, but the tower was reduced in height by almost a metre in the nineteenth century, when it was reused as a belfry and a door was inserted at ground level in a blocked-up gap in the masonry. In 1909 the Office of Public Works filled in this doorway, and in 1973 the interior was cleared out and other repairs were done, including work to the raised doorway.

In the Middle Ages this was the site of the parish church, listed in the 1302–6 papal taxation, and some architectural details from a medieval church are exhibited close to the tower. The nineteenth-century Church of Ireland parish church (now a folk museum) may occupy the site of an earlier church or churches.

Local folklore claims that a woman with three aprons full of stones built the round tower and that she built it in one night. One third of the stones was said to be underground, one third is still visible above ground and the remaining third has disappeared over the years. In the bed of the Fane River can be seen a very large bare footprint said to belong to the mystery woman.

It is said that the Danes attacked the monastery many times. In one of the last great battles between the Danes and the Irish, two Danes, a father and son, were captured by the victorious Irish army. They demanded to know the Danish secret of making wine from heather. The father asked the Irish to kill his son, promising that he would then tell them the secret. But when the son was killed the father told his captors to do the same to him; then the secret would never be told. He was put to death and both are buried nearby in Dunelty Bog.

Sources: *UJA* 5, 1857, 116-21; Livingstone P., 1980, 10, 19, 25-9, 570-1; *AICM* 1986, 86; Duffy P.J., 1993, 98-9; Lalor B., 1999, 204-6; Murphy M.J., 1975, 147.

47 INISHKEEN MOTTE AND BAILEY

MONUMENT TYPE	Motte, Bailey and Bawn
LOCATION	Inishkeen village, next to Patrick Kavanagh Centre
GRID REFERENCE	H933 068
MONUMENT NUMBER	MN29:3301
STATUS	Recorded Historic Monument

Situated on the outskirts of Inishkeen in Patrick Kavanagh country, this large, impressive tree-covered motte with traces of a bailey commands extensive views over the drumlins of south Monaghan. The motte was once part of a series of earthen fortifications built as the Normans attempted to advance into Ulster in the thirteenth century.

The motte is flat-topped and the surrounding ditch is visible except at the east side. Local tradition relates the finding of a 'passage lined with stones

'The little fort, where fairies sport, in lovely Inishkeen'

and covered with large flags' in the motte, which may indicate a
souterrain or a burial mound. An account of this story appears in the
JRSAI (Journal of the Royal Society of Antiquaries of Ireland) of 1875,
which also reports the discovery of a recess or small chamber in the side of
the passage, which contained 'a well'. There are traces of an oval bailey on the
east side of the mound.

The bawn, later in date, is located immediately northeast of the bailey. The bawn is rectangular and its walls are constructed of rough stone. It is entered by a large arch and inside are the foundations of a gatehouse. As at Faughart (38) and Louth (36), Inishkeen motte has an ancient church foundation in its immediate vicinity (46). There are many stories about the motte, about ghosts and the occupation of the motte and bailey by fairies.

> Grasslike shades and branches green
> The Fane rolled on between,
> So clear and bright, like stars at night,
> Through lovely Inishkeen.
> The water mill, beneath your hill,
> The Round Tower's holy head.
> Time never marred, it seems to guard,
> The old home of the dead.
> School house nigh, two stories high,
> The haunted mount so green,
> The little fort, where fairies sport,
> In lovely Inishkeen.
> The chapel store lie o'er the clay,
> With these beneath the day,
> You can see the antique tombstones of brown and grey.
> The Church of Bess, now in distress,
> Where weeds and grass are green.
> And growing there men knelt in prayer,
> In lovely Inishkeen.
> (From the ballad *Lovely Inishkeen*, Irish Folklore Collection,
> reprinted in *Along the Black Pig's Dyke,* Castleblaney 1993, 165)

Sources: *AICM* 1986, 90; pl 6.; Duffy P.J., 1993, 98-9.

48 MANNAN CASTLE

MONUMENT TYPE	Motte, Baileys and Castle
LOCATION	South of Donaghmoyne village, in Donaghmoyne golf-course
GRID REFERENCE	H854 074
MONUMENT NUMBER	MN28:118
STATUS	National Monument No.382

The tree-covered hilltop conceals the Motte, Baileys and stone Castle

Mannan Castle – *Caisleán Mhannain* – is an extremely large motte with two baileys, located on the summit of a drumlin hill overlooking the south Monaghan drumlin landscape. Set in the middle of the new Donaghmoyne golf course, the tree-covered motte commands extensive views over south-east Ulster.

Peter Pipard, an Anglo-Norman knight, probably began to build

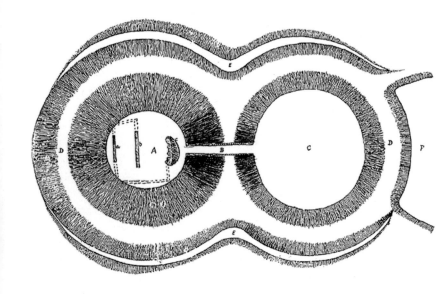

Mannan Castle, Donaghmoyne – after CLAJ, 1910

the castle in about 1193 and at first it is likely to have been wooden. A stone castle was erected in 1244 and the motte was joined to the castle by means of a stone causeway or bridge, probably at the same time. The castle was ceded to the Crown in 1302 and then leased at a nominal rent to other Anglo-Norman families, first to the Clintons and then to the Gernons, but by the fifteenth century it had been abandoned.

The motte is covered with trees, but large fragments of masonry from the castle walls are visible on the site. According to the historian and antiquarian E P Shirley, there was a 'tall arch' standing on the motte in 1843, but unfortunately this and other remains of the buildings have been vandalised in the past.

Tradition records a conflict between Pipard and the Bishop of Ardee, Tiarnach Mac Giolla Ronain, over the construction of the castle. It is said that the bishop asked workmen to stop building the castle and when they refused he threw himself into a trench in front of them. The work was halted until Pipard returned to the site and dragged the bishop out of the trench. Mac Giolla Ronain cursed him and vowed that the Pipard family would not keep the land on which the castle was built. The story goes that Pipard was struck down with leprosy and died.

Three pools are associated with Mannan Castle. Local folklore claims that the wealth of Mannan is lying at the bottom of one of the pools, and it can only be removed at certain times and under certain conditions. One of these conditions requires the treasure to be removed using four 'pure white' horses. It is said that one night treasure-hunters, accompanied by the required four white horses, arrived in search of the hidden trove. They found the chain that holds the treasure together and attached it to the horses. The horses pulled with all their might and the treasure began to rise. But, just as the hoard reached the surface of the water, the chain broke and the treasure sank back into the murky depths of the pool. On closer examination it was found that one of the horses had a black hair!

Sources: *CLAJ* 1910, 62; *AICM* 1986, 91; Duffy P.J., 1993, 91-2.

ABBREVIATIONS

ASCL 1991 An Archaeological Survey of County Louth, Buckley V.M. & Sweetman P.D., Dublin, 1991.

AICM 1986 An Archaeological Inventory of County Monaghan, Brindley A., Dublin, 1986.

ASCD 1966 An Archaeological Survey of County Down, Belfast, HMSO, 1966.

CLAJ County Louth Archaeological Journal

DOENI (EHS)Department of the Environment for Northern Ireland (Environment and Heritage Service)

HMSO Her Majesty's Stationery Office

PBNHPS Proceedings of the Nat. History and Phil. Society 2nd Series 1., Belfast, 1938.

PSAMNI 1940 A Preliminary Survey of the Ancient Monuments of Northern Ireland, Ed. Chart D.A., Belfast, 1940.

UJA Ulster Journal of Archaeology

GENERAL BIBLIOGRAPHY

Aalen F.H.A., Whelan K., Stout M., Atlas of the Irish Rural Landscape, Cork, 1997.

Arthurs J.B., 'Sliabh Fuaid', Bulletin of the Ulster Place-Name Society, 2, 1954, 33-8.

Barrow G.L., The Round Towers of Ireland, Dublin, 1976.

Bell J., A letter from Mr J.Bell, Newry Magazine 2, Newry, 1816, 234-40.

Borlase, The Dolmens of Ireland, Dublin, 1976.

Brett C.E.B., Buildings of County Armagh, Belfast, 1999.

Carville G., Creggan: A Celtic Christian Site, Dundalk, 1996.

Clarke G. & O'Sullivan H., Dundalk and North Louth, Paintings and Stories from Cú Chulainn's Country, Cottage Publications, 1997.

Collins A.E.P., Ballykeel Dolmen and Cairn, Ulster Journal of Archaeology, Vol 28, 1965, 47-70.

Collins A.E.P. & Wilson B.C.S., The Slieve Gullion Cairns, Co Armagh, Ulster Journal of Archaeology, Vol 26, 1963, 19-40.

Collins A.E.P. & Wilson B.C.S., Excavation of a court cairn at Ballymacdermot, Co Armagh, Ulster Journal of Archaeology, Vol 27, 1964, 3-22.

Coote C., A Statistical Survey of the county of Armagh, with observations on the means of improvement, Dublin, 1804.

Cowan J.D., An Irish Parish, Past and Present, being the parish of Donaghmore, Co Down, London, 1914.

Crawford S., Mourne Rambles, A Cusle na nGael Supplement, Newry, 1994.

Crawford M.G., Legendary Stories of the Carlingford Lough District, Newry, 1996.

Crowe W.H., The Ring of Mourne, Dundalk, 1969.

Davies O., Corliss Fort, County Louth Archaeology Journal, Vol 4, 1940.

Davies O. & Paterson T.G.F., Excavations at Clontygora Large Cairn, Co Armagh, Proceedings of Nat. History & Phil. Society 2nd Series 1, 1938, 20-42.

Donaldson J., A Historical and Statistical Account of the Barony of the Upper Fews in the County of Armagh (1838), Dundalk, 1923.

Donnelly C.J., Living Places: Archaeology, Continuity and Change at Historic Monuments in Northern Ireland, Belfast, 1997.

Duffy P.J., Landscapes of South Ulster, An Atlas of the Diocese of Clogher, Belfast, 1993.

Evans E.E., Mourne Country, Landscape in South Down, Dundalk, 1951.

Evans E.E., Prehistoric and Early Christian Ireland: a guide, London, 1966.

Fitzpatrick W.J., An Old Timer Talking, Reminiscences and Stories, Kilkeel, 1963.

From the Isles of the North: early medieval art in Ireland and Britain, Ed. Burke C., Belfast, 1995.

Gaskell-Brown C., Greencastle, Ulster Journal of Archaeology, Vol 42, 1979, 51-65.

Glassie H., Passing the Time, Folklore and History of an Ulster Community, Dublin, 1982.

Gwynn A. & Hadcock R.N., Medieval Religious Houses: Ireland, London, 1970.

Hamlin A., The Blackwater Group of Crosses, From the Isles of the North, Ed. Burke, Belfast, 1995, 187-96.

Hamlin A. and Lynn C., Pieces of the Past: Archaeological Excavations by the Department of the Environment for Northern Ireland 1970–1986, Belfast, 1988.

Harbison P., Guide to the National and Historic Monuments of Ireland, Dublin, 1992.

Harbison P., The High Crosses of Ireland: an iconographical and photographic survey, 2 Vols, Bonn, 1992.

Hayes-McCoy G.A., Ulster and Other Maps c.1600, Dublin, 1964.

Herity M. & Eoghan G., Ireland in Pre-history, London, 1977.

Historical Sketches of Tynan and Middletown, Ed. Seamus Mallon, Tynan, 1995.

Hynes J. & Campbell M., Armagh City of Light and Learning, Paintings and Stories from the Orchard County, Cottage Publications, 1997.

HMSO Historic Monuments of Northern Ireland, Belfast, 1987. (revised edition forthcoming in 2001)

Jefferies H.A., Rev. William Reeves 'Sites of Ancient Churches in the County of Armagh, December 1879' Seanchas Ard Mhacha, Vol 17, 1996-7, 194-7.

Keating J., Journal of Keady and District Historical Society, Monaghan, 1992.

Lalor, 1999, Lalor B., The Irish Round Tower, Origins and Architecture Explored, Cork, 1999.

Leask H.G., Irish Churches and Monastic Buildings, Dundalk, 1955.

Lewis S., A Topographical Dictionary of Ireland, 3 Vols, London, 1837.

Livingston P., The Monaghan Story, Monaghan, 1980.

Lynn C.J., The Kings Stables, Ulster Journal of Archaeology, Vol 30, 1977, 42-62.

Manning C., JCLAS 23, 1996.

MacNeill M., The Festival of Lughnasa, Dublin, 1982.

Mc Kay P., A Dictionary of Ulster Place-Names, Belfast, 1999.

McNeill T., Castles in Ireland, Feudal Power in a Celtic World, Routledge, 1997.

Mallory J.P., Navan Fort, The Ancient Capital of Ulster, Ulster Archaeological Society, 1993.

Morris H., Mannan Castle, CLAJ Vol.11, 1910-11, 262-70.

Murphy M.J., Now You're Talking ... Folktales from the North of Ireland, Dundalk, 1975.

Murphy M.J., Sayings and Stories from Slieve Gullion, Dundalk, 1990.

Murphy M.J., At Slieve Gullion's Foot, Dundalk, 1990.

O'Donovan J., Letters containing information relative to the antiquities of the counties of Armagh and Monaghan collected during Ordnance Survey in 1835, Ed. M. O'Flanagan, Bray, 1927.

Ó Mainnín M.B., Place-Names of Northern Ireland III, The Mournes, Belfast, 1993.

Ó hÓgáin D., Myth, Legend and Romance, an Encyclopedia of Mythology and Folklore, New York, 1991.

Paterson T.G.F., County Cracks, Old Tales from the County of Armagh, Dundalk, 1945.

Paterson T.G.F., Harvest Home, The Last Sheaf, Dundalk, 1975.

Reeves W., Eccelestical Antiquities of Down, Connor, and Dromore, Dublin, 1847.

Reeves W., The Kilnasaggart Pillar Stone, Ulster Journal of Archaeology, 1853.

Roe H.M., Seanchas Ard Mhacha, 1955.

Sherry B., Along the Black Pig's Dyke, Folklore from Monaghan and South Armagh, Castleblaney, 1993.

Stout M., The Irish Ringfort, Dublin, 1997.

Stuart J., Historical Memoirs of the city of Armagh, Newry, 1819.

Toner G. and Ó Mainnín M.B., Place-Names of Northern Ireland I, Newry and South-West Down, Belfast, 1992.

Tempest H.G., Gossiping Guide to County Louth Pt 1, Castletown to Omeath, Dundalk, 1952.

Tempest H.G., Gossiping Guide to County Louth Pt 11, Ravensdale to Channonrock, Dundalk, 1952.

Waterman D.M. & Collins A.E.P., Greencastle, Ulster Journal of Archaeology, Vol 15, 1952, 211-19.

Waterman D.M., A Guide to Narrowater Castle, HMSO, Belfast, 1962.

Waterman D.M., The court cairn at Annaghmare, Ulster Journal of Archaeology, Vol 28, 1965, 3-46.

Waterman D.M., Excavations at Navan Fort 1961-71, Belfast, 1997 (Ed. Lynn C.J.).

THE O'BRIEN PRESS
CITY GUIDES SERIES

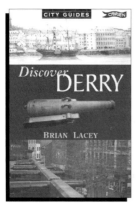

DISCOVER DERRY
Brian Lacey

This book tells the fascinating story of Derry, in words and pictures, from the sixth century to the present day. Part one explores the history of Derry through key events, including the founding of the Early Christian Church, the first English invasion in 1566, the Apprentice Boys' rebellion and the Troubles of the twentieth century. Part two visits Derry's most interesting buildings and landmarks, including: the city walls, the Guildhall, the Memorial Hall, St Columb's Cathedral, Magee College and the Quayside.

Paperback £9.99/€12.68/$16.95

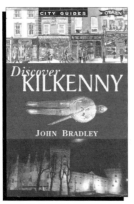

DISCOVER KILKENNY
John Bradley

Kilkenny has long been noted as Ireland's foremost medieval town. This is the story of its long and fascinating history. Part one explores the history of Kilkenny through key events, including the founding of the Early Christian monastery, the coming of the Normans and the witchcraft trial of Alice Kyteler. Part two visits Kilkenny's most interesting buildings and landmarks, including Kilkenny Castle, St Canice's Cathedral and Rothe House.

Paperback £9.99/€12.68/$16.95

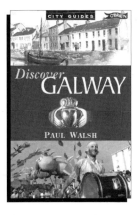

DISCOVER GALWAY
Paul Walsh

Galway is a vibrant, exuberant place with a tangible charm. This book presents the history of this unique city. Part one explores the history of the city, which spans almost ten centuries, including the lives of the townspeople, the architecture of the buildings, religion and politics and development in modern times. Part two provides a guide to the historic places and buildings, including St Nicholas's Church, Lynch's and Blake's Castles, the Cathedral, Eyre Square, the Spanish Arch and Fish Market and the Claddagh.

Paperback £9.99/€12.68/$16.95

DISCOVER WATERFORD

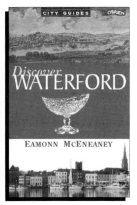

Eamonn McEneaney

Waterford is the oldest centre of continuous urban settlement in Ireland. It is Ireland's oldest city outdating all of the northern European capitals except London and Paris. *Discover Waterford* provides all the information a tourist needs: an overview of the city's history since it's foundation in 914 AD by a Viking pirate, and a guide to all the main historical buildings that a tourist will come across as they walk around the city.

Paperback £9.99/€12.68/$16.95

THE GOLDEN BOOK OF IRELAND
Frances Power

Over 200 stunning original photographs of Ireland, North and South, featuring its historic places, monuments, breathtaking scenery, the people, fairs and festivals. Each photograph is accompanied by fact-filled, informative text on the history, legend, lives and customs covered by the pictures. The book takes you on a county by county tour of Ireland, visiting all the major tourist attractions, as well as illustrating unique features for which the Irish landscape is famous, such as thatched cottages, stone walls and round towers. Also available in French, German, Italian and Spanish.

Paperback £8.99/€11.41/$12.95

Send for our full-colour catalogue